People all over the world are suffering from the effects of air pollution, contaminated land, polluted water and polluted food; toxic substances are being dumped in 'time-bomb' landfill sites that threaten water supplies for hundreds or thousands of years; our seas are polluted; and now, to cap it all, the global environment we depend on is at risk from climate change and ozone depletion – and all because of pollution.

The good news is that there is a solution – and we all have a part to play in it. In the last 100 years of life on earth we have done enormous damage to the planet but it is not irreversible. And in the last 10 we have gone further to slow down our polluting ways than ever before. The planet can heal itself, but we have to let that happen . . .

Caroline Clayton is a freelance journalist and writer on environmental issues. She is the author of several books, including *Causing a Stink! The Eco-Warrior's Handbook*.

Friends of the Earth is the UK's most influential environmental pressure group and campaigns on a wide range of pollution issues.

Dirty Planet

The Friends of the Earth Guide to Pollution and What You Can Do About It

Caroline Clayton

FRIENDS *of the*
earth
for the planet for people

Livewire
from The Women's Press

First published by Livewire Books, The Women's Press Ltd, 2000
A member of the Namara Group
34 Great Sutton Street, London EC1V 0LQ

British Library Cataloguing-in-Publication Data
A catalogue record for this book is available from the British Library.

ISBN 0 7043 4964 7

Typeset in 12/14pt Bembo by FSH Ltd, London
Printed and bound in Great Britain by Cox & Wyman Ltd, Reading,
Berkshire

Contents

Acknowledgements

Enormous thanks to everyone who helped put this book together, including

Jean McNeil, Andy Neather, Neil Verlander, Adeela Warley, Mike Childs, Tony Bosworth, Roger Higman, Dr Anna Thomas, Dr Michael Warhurst, Anna Stanford, Pad Green at Friends of the Earth, Mandy Garnett at FOE Bristol, The Women's Environmental Network, Surfers Against Sewage, National Asthma Campaign, Charlotte Cole at The Women's Press, Ralph Minor, Kevin Mearns, Natalia Khazan, Maria Coryell-Martin, Nicola Bunt, Kruti Parekh, Theresia van der Merwe and Gemma Smith.

Introduction

Fact: **Since 1900, global sea levels have risen by between 10 and 25cm, which is significantly higher than the rate averaged over the last several thousand years.**

Fact: **Cancer in children under 15 has risen by 10 per cent between 1974 and 1991 in the US, while cases of the most common leukaemia, acute lymphoblastic leukaemia, rose by 1 per cent per year in the US between 1973 and 1994. Brain tumour rates have gone up by 2 per cent per year.**

Fact: **In the UK in 1993 GPS recorded five times as many new cases of asthma in pre-school children as they had in 1979.**

Fact: **During the last 20 to 40 years in Denmark, Sweden, Germany, Norway, Finland, Canada and the US, there have been more female births than would normally be expected to occur.**

Fact: **It is not just humans and animals that are being affected. Our architectural heritage is crumbling. In the last 50 years ancient statues in Rome have become more damaged than they have over the previous 2000 years. The Taj Mahal in India, once shimmering white marble, is now yellowed, crumbling and pock-marked.**

Question: **What do these disturbing things that are occurring all around the planet have in common?** Answer: **They are caused by soaring levels of environmental pollution.**

Pollution is a global problem that no one on Planet Earth today can escape. And some of us are more responsible for it than others. In the developed West we enjoy the benefits of much more than our fair share of the world's energy – and yet the whole planet carries the burden of our polluting emissions.

Pollution is one of the most pressing issues of today; as the developing world expands, pollution is set to reach crisis proportions. Over the last few centuries the world has transformed dramatically from a remote collection of agricultural-based civilisations into a global 'village' dominated by powerful industrialised manufacturing nations. As nations continue to develop, the global demand for electricity and cars continues to rise – particularly in China, with 1205 million people the most populous country on the planet – and the resulting vast increase in pollution will have dramatic consequences for the planet's ecosystem.

As you read through the chapters that follow you'll get an idea of the extent of pollution and how it now affects all areas of our life and even the remotest parts of the planet. But don't be too disheartened; you'll also find plenty of practical solutions to make things change. You can make a difference. Just read on.

Chapter 1
Air Pollution

Fact: In India's main cities, Delhi and Bombay, breathing the air is the equivalent of smoking 10–20 cigarettes a day and in Delhi alone 7500 people die every year of respiratory illness.

Fact: In Milan, Italy an after-Christmas smoke fog caused the city's cashpoint machines to refuse to pay out money. They were so clogged up by pollution from traffic that the machines couldn't read the cards' magnetic strips.

Fact: In the Czech Republic heating plants sometimes have to stop producing hot water for apartments when sulphur-dioxide levels rise to as much as four times those allowed by law.

Fact: Air pollution triggers 1 in 50 heart attacks in London.

Fact: In Beijing and other cities where air pollution is very bad, entrepreneurs have spotted a market opportunity: opening up 'oxygen bars' where you can sit and rent an oxygen mask to recover. The Dreamland Oxygen Bar in Beijing serves up a pure oxygen 'drink'. £3.75 buys you half an hour of pure oxygen; for £6 you get a special 'cocktail' with Chinese herbal remedies. You sit and sip a cold drink with a tube up your nose and a small oxygen canister in front of you.

These frightening facts about air pollution are enough to leave you gasping. Air pollution is something we should all be worried about because none of us can escape it entirely. Air pollution doesn't just vanish into thin air; it lingers in the atmosphere or gets carried by the wind to

3

another part of the world to pollute someone else's patch. In fact, even the remotest parts of the planet – the North and South Poles – are affected by pollution. On days when there is little or no wind, pollution gets trapped in the atmosphere. Smogs – visible hazes or fogs of deadly chemicals – are perhaps the most obvious evidence of air pollution. Once confined to notoriously polluted cities such as Los Angeles and Athens, smogs now occur regularly in the UK. And they don't affect just our busiest cities; they are a growing problem in parts of the countryside, too.

This chapter takes a long look at air pollution, what's causing it and how it can affect us. It also explains lots of things we can do to make a difference, so that we can all breathe a little easier.

What's polluting our air?

There are a number of different types of air pollutants, all of which affect our health differently. If you live in an area with poor air quality, then every time you breathe in – that's around 30,000 times a day – you'll be breathing in a lungful of dirty, polluted air. The effects of this vary from person to person, but if you're exposed long enough you will start feeling tired and short of breath. After all, your body will be getting less oxygen than it needs to keep you in tiptop condition. The delicate lining of your respiratory tract – your nose, throat and chest – might get irritated and inflamed. Sore throats, sore, runny noses, headaches, hoarseness or voice loss, wheezing, coughing, breathing difficulties and chest pain...these can all be side-effects of air pollution.

The list that follows details the main types of air pollutants, how they get released into the atmosphere and how they each affect our health. Naturally in everyday life you don't breathe in just one of these pollutants. Every lungful of air contains a potentially deadly cocktail of pollution. And, worse still, many scientists believe that there is a combined effect from the pollutants working together; breathing in one pollutant weakens the body's resistance to the effects of another. Now that is scary.

Pollutant: CARBON MONOXIDE

Where it comes from: motor vehicles and power stations burning fossil fuels such as coal, oil and gas. Ninety-nine per cent of the carbon monoxide found in London's air is caused by traffic.

Too much makes us ill because it reduces the ability of the blood to carry oxygen, which it needs to keep your body working properly. It causes headaches, drowsiness and could even be fatal.

Pollutant: SULPHUR DIOXIDE (SO_2)

Where it comes from: three-quarters of all SO_2 emissions in the UK come from our coal-burning power stations. The rest comes from exhaust fumes, particularly diesel engines.

Too much makes us ill because it can cause lung and breathing problems and a heavy cough. And too much SO_2 makes rainwater 'acid'. Acid rain contaminates rivers, streams and lakes, killing surrounding wildlife and threatening the food-chain. Acid rain is also seriously eroding buildings, especially historical monuments. For example, if you touched the Parthenon, the great monument of ancient Greece – which, made of solid white marble, has survived invasions and bombs – your finger would come away with a coating of soft, sugary pumice.

Pollutant: NITROGEN OXIDES (nitrogen dioxide and nitric oxide)

Where it comes from: half of the excess nitrogen oxides in our air comes from traffic fumes. A quarter of it comes from power stations.

Too many make us ill because they reduce our resistance to infection, irritate the lungs and aggravate asthma. They also cause acid rain and smogs.

Pollutant: OZONE

Where it comes from: ozone is produced as a result of other gases (such as nitrogen oxides and hydrocarbons) mixing together, and so it is known as a secondary pollutant. Ozone is safe high in the sky, but not at ground level.

Too much makes us ill because it can harm throats, lungs and immune systems and damage crops and plants. In 1996 one of the worst readings in the UK for low-level ozone was 130 per cent higher than the government's proposed safe limit.

Pollutant: VOCS (volatile organic compounds, also known as hydrocarbons)

Where they come from: mainly from traffic exhaust fumes and also from industrial processes and solvents.

Too many make us ill because they cause smogs. Benzene, which escapes from petrol tanks and pumps during refuelling, is particularly dangerous because it can cause leukaemia.

Pollutant: PARTICULATES

Where they come from: these are the tiny black dots of soot given off in diesel exhaust fumes.

Too many make us ill because they can pass into the lungs and choke them. They make breathing problems such as asthma much worse. Scientists researching into particulates have found a link between particle levels and death rates. In other words, as levels of particulates in the air rise, so too do death rates. It is possible that over 10,000 people die prematurely every year because of this one pollutant. There is no safe level of this pollutant. And the truth is that we don't yet know how harmful particulates are to our health.

Pollutant: DIOXINS

Where they come from: they are released into the air when chlorine-containing materials, such as PVC plastic or some sanitary towels and tampons, are burnt. Hospital incinerators are a large source because hospitals use PVC in supposedly 'disposable' equipment. Airborne dioxins can be breathed in but may also fall on agricultural land where animals such as cows eat grass and plants contaminated by them. The dioxins stick firmly to the fat in the cow, particularly to the milk fat and to the fatty part of the meat. Since they do not break down, animals carrying dioxins in their fat are actually acting as dioxin 'concentrators'. Eating animal fat is the major source of dioxins for humans.

Too many make us ill because, even at very low levels, they are extremely toxic. They take a very long time to break down, either in the body or in the environment. They are particularly dangerous because of their ability to accumulate within the food–chain and people's bodies (there's more about this in chapter four). Dioxins have been linked with cancer and hormonal effects such as reduced sperm counts in men and endometriosis in women (a condition where tissue that lines the womb starts growing around the ovaries and fallopian tubes, causing fertility problems). Dioxins can also affect the immune system and foetal development. An industrial accident in Seveso, Italy released large amounts of dioxin into the atmosphere. In the eight years after the accident twelve daughters and no sons were born to nine couples with the highest dioxin exposure: statistics that defy the norm.

Pollutant: LEAD
Where it comes from: traffic fumes.

Too much makes us ill because it is a heavy metal and can accumulate in the human body. Lead is particularly harmful because it damages the body's central nervous system and can retard young children's brain power. Children are three times more at risk from the damaging effects of lead than adults because their nervous systems are still developing. Lead is still a problem as lots of cars run on leaded petrol.

As bad as it gets

Given the list of serious health effects that all these pollutants can cause, it is no wonder that when air-pollution levels are high hospital admissions go up.

Fifty years ago the air quality in the UK was a very serious problem. This was mainly because factories were allowed to pump out polluting fumes and also because, in those days, more people burnt coal fires to heat their homes. In December 1952 a cloud of thick, smoky smog settled on London. It was extremely cold and the poisonous smog stayed around for four days. In the weeks that followed, London's death rate soared and it is now reckoned that at least 4000 people died because of this single episode of air pollution!

One positive effect of this disastrous smog was that the government passed the Clean Air Act (1956) and many towns and cities were made smoke-free zones. But in the 50 years since, air pollution has again become nearly as big a problem as it once was, because of the fumes pumped out of power stations and the ever-increasing numbers of cars and lorries on our roads. Traffic pollution hit an all-time peak in 1993 just before it became compulsory for all new cars to be fitted with fume-reducing catalytic convertors. Since then pollution levels have been gradually reducing but they are not falling fast enough. Indeed, if the number of cars continues to grow unchecked, pollution levels will be on the rise again! We can't allow this to happen. Already every year in the UK up to 24,000 people die before their time because of air pollution.

Of course, the air-pollution problem in the UK reflects what is happening all around the world. Globally, air quality has deteriorated as the world has become industrialised. Large cities with high concentrations of cars, industry and people tend to have the highest levels of air pollution.

Mexico City, which has a population of 26 million people, has one of the worst air-pollution problems in the world. It is set in a basin surrounded by mountains and in winter cold air hangs over the city, preventing the hotter air from cars and factories from rising. The polluted air lingers, on bad days turning the city into what Mexican scientists call a 'toxic gas chamber'. In 1988 smog in Mexico caused some people to faint in the street. And when the air gets particularly smoggy, small birds have been known to drop unconscious from the trees!

It's the old and the very young who are particularly vulnerable to 'air-pollution diseases' such as chest infections and asthma. The Mexican authorities are so concerned about pollution that they are thinking about delaying the start of the school day until 10 am to spare children from the worst of the smog. They've even thought about shifting the school holiday from July to December, so children can have a chance to get out of the city during the winter, when the air quality is at its worst.

Air pollution and asthma

Asthma is an age-old condition. The ancient Egyptians used to treat it with crocodile dung, so it's certainly been around since long before cars were invented. Today, however, it is a growing problem: one in seven children in the UK now has asthma. Scientists can't say for sure why the incidence of this condition is on the increase. But Friends of the Earth (FOE) believes it is no coincidence that the incidence of asthma has more than doubled in the last 15 years in line with increased road traffic.

Asthma causes the air passages in the lungs to become narrower, making it difficult to breathe. It is linked to not one, but many triggers such as viral infections, vigorous exercise, pets, cold weather and even prolonged laughing!

Some women find their asthma gets worse in the last few days before their period. Air pollution is a trigger, too. For example, children with asthma whose parents smoke have more severe symptoms. And children living in urban areas, fugged up with traffic fumes, suffer more. In some inner-city areas one child in three is asthmatic.

Summer and winter smogs are bad news for anyone who suffers from asthma. In severe smogs asthma sufferers often have no choice but to stay indoors. That means they can't go to school or work and they miss out on life! But ultimately we all lose. If you're asthmatic yourself you'll know what it's like to have to stay off the scene when it's smoggy. And even if you don't suffer yourself, you may well lose an asthmatic friend's company when air quality gets particularly bad. The National Asthma Campaign has estimated that asthma costs the UK over £1 billion each year in terms of the cost of health care and days off sick.

FOE believes that everyone – young, old, asthmatic or otherwise – has an absolute right to cleaner air, which means that each and every one of us should clean up our acts!

The National Asthma Campaign runs an asthma helpline to answer any queries you, your friends or family may have about asthma. (See 'Hot Contacts!' on page 145.)

Ill winds blow no good

We've all got to make a fuss about air pollution. Even if the pollutants we're producing over here eventually disperse, they move on to take effect elsewhere on earth.

Vast amounts of UK pollution are responsible for the acid rain that falls on Scandinavia, for example. And just to prove that what goes around comes around, the south east of Britain receives similarly high levels of ozone, blown over from continental Europe.

Air quality and standards

Recently the UK government has recognised that the public wants better information on pollution. It has improved air monitoring and set up a free phone line and web site to give out up-to-the-minute information. The government lets the media know when pollution is particularly bad so that those most at risk will hear of it and can stay indoors until it passes.

In March 1997 the UK government introduced new limits on air pollution that must be met by the year 2005. These limits are tougher than previous standards and have been set by a team of air-pollution scientists and health experts. The team looked at all levels of all types of pollutants and between them agreed a 'safe' level for most types of pollutants.

Nearly a third of the UK population lives in areas where air pollution exceeds these new safety levels. It is up to local authorities (councils) to put the brakes on air pollution – and quickly. Each and every council in the land is duty-bound to make sure that by the year 2005 pollution in its area doesn't exceed permitted levels. The standards vary from one pollutant to another and there are a few special exceptions. For example, ozone can exceed the recommended safe level for 10 days each year.

In theory things are looking good. Friends of the Earth believes these new limits go a long way to making air clean and safe to breathe. If we meet them, we'll all breathe easier.

Pollution busters!

What you can do

The pollution solution is set to happen: from councils acting locally, from the government at a national level and from the EC to protect us at a European level. But the louder we all call and the harder we all push for action, the quicker it will come. Here's a list of pollution-busting measures to get you started.

Keep tabs on your local air quality. You can check it out:
- by phone. Call the Department of the Environment's Pollution Help Line for free on 0800 556677
- on CEEFAX (pages 410–417) or TELETEXT (page 106)
- by logging on to the Department of the Environment's web site. The address is http://www.open.gov.uk/doe/envir

If air quality stays poor, let your local community know about it! Write to your local paper and/or MP about your concerns. Enclose a photo to illustrate your point. For example, if you are asthmatic and want to see a reduction in traffic, ask a friend to photograph you with your inhaler alongside a busy road.

Write to your local council. Ask it if it is meeting the government's new standards on air pollution. If not, ask it what's in its action plan to make sure it's on target for 2005.

Keep an eye out for black smoke – black as opposed to a greyish or whitish colour. Black smoke of any kind is illegal, for example, burning fields of straw is banned. You should report any sightings to the Environment Agency on 0800 807060.

Later on in this book we'll be looking at industry and how it causes air (and other types of) pollution. But as cars are the biggest (and growing) cause of air pollution, they've a chapter of their very own coming up next. We've got to curb our car use and rethink ways of getting about if air pollution is to improve. There are loads of ways you can help do this, described in chapter two.

Natalia Khazan is 17 and lives in Dnepropetrovsk, one of the Ukraine's biggest industrial towns. Her life has been directly affected by air pollution but she is determined to do something about it.

'My town is a major industrial centre for chemicals, clothing, power and even space-rocket plants that pump out a lethal cocktail of noxious fumes. The atmosphere here is now being increasingly poisoned by growing amounts of road traffic; our people are buying more cars than ever before, mainly second-hand ones from western Europe with particularly poor and polluting exhausts.

'In fact local air pollution from cars has begun to exceed industrial pollution. Enormous amounts of sulphur dioxide, carbon monoxide and nitrogen oxide in the atmosphere are harming our health, particularly women's reproductive health.

'Five years ago I joined the Youth Environmental League of Prydneprovye (MELP for short) to campaign for cleaner air. We met with the local authorities and representatives of central government, with academics and environmental officers, eco-groups and activists, and with ordinary people from all areas of the town. We pinpointed companies making huge profits by saving on environmental safety at the expense of the town's health. We spread the word through local TV and papers. Eventually one of the most popular local papers agreed to print regular information on air pollution in all areas of the town.

'We know that the root causes of air pollution lie in the town's industrial structure, in its outdated plants and coal-fired industry. Plant managers don't have the money or the incentive to reconstruct the plants. In fact, right now, they're more worried about losing their jobs in the poor economic climate. But thanks to our campaign and the local authority's efforts the pollution problem here has improved: an air-monitoring system has been introduced, some plants have been equipped to reduce their noxious emissions and legal limits on car exhausts may be introduced. Monitoring devices have shown – and our own noses can confirm – that the air is getting a little cleaner. But we've still got a long way to go.'

Chapter 2
The Trouble with Traffic

Fact: **In half of the world's megacities (that's a city with more than 10 million people) motor vehicles are the biggest source of pollution. In London there are nearly 2.3 million cars; that's one for every three inhabitants of the city.**

Fact: **Cars and other motor vehicles are the fastest growing source of carbon dioxide in the UK today. Each car produces four times its own weight of carbon dioxide in a year.**

Fact: **Traffic fumes contain some of the most harmful substances – benzene is one – known to medical science.**

Fact: **There are now 480 million cars polluting this planet and almost 29 million new cars are manufactured each year.**

Fact: **Making an average car produces 54 tonnes of waste.**

Chapter one has pointed out the bad news: air, that serious stuff of life, is being seriously polluted. Chapter two has some more shocking news: measures to contain air pollution will never work as long as we keep turning up the choke and relying on our cars to go from A to B.

More and more of our everyday journeys – even the shortest of trips that could be easily walked or cycled – are now made by car. Almost one in three journeys under five miles in big cities are made by car. Out of town that figure increases to one in two short journeys being made by car. And less than 3 per cent of all short journeys are made by bicycle. As a comparison the Dutch, who have much better cycling facilities, make almost 40 per cent of short journeys by bike and only one in five journeys by car.

Just over 100 years ago there were only a handful of cars (or 'horseless carriages') on our roads (actually there weren't many roads either), and even Jeremy Clarkson couldn't enthuse about their top speeds (just slightly above a snail's pace). Interestingly, although cars look very different today, they still crawl along our city streets at the same speed as a horse and cart. Traffic speeds in London average 16km per hour, just as they did 100 years ago!

Despite this we've turned the car into an icon; the more flashy the car, the better person we are seen to be! But the truth is we've gone car mad and our four-wheel dependency is costing us the earth – literally.

The world's gone car-azy!

Fifty years ago there were just 2.3 million cars on the road. Only 30 years ago this figure had increased to 11 million. The number of cars has almost doubled since then; in the UK today there are over 21 million cars on the road. And it's not just here; this massive explosion in car numbers is a worldwide phenomenon.

Most of the world's cars (80 per cent) are owned by less than 20 per cent of its people, mainly those in richer nations. There are more cars in just one US city – greater Los Angeles – than in the whole of India, China, Indonesia, Pakistan and Bangladesh put together. But the worrying news is that in developing countries car numbers are now increasing at a faster rate than in the West. In Karachi, Pakistan, for example, the car population is growing 2.5 times faster than the human population and it has one of the most severe air-pollution problems in the world.

Cars are killers

We know that air pollution from exhaust fumes can trigger asthma and create havoc with our health. But cars don't just leave us gasping. Road traffic kills 3600 people each year and leaves 320,000 others injured.

Being killed in a road accident is the most common cause of death in the under-15s. Roughly 1 child in 15 is injured in a road accident before his or her 16th birthday. Imagine a group of 15 of your school friends as part of that statistic – it doesn't bear thinking about!

Then there's the harm that cars do to our wildlife. It's reckoned that at least 47,000 badgers are killed each year by cars – that's one from every family of badgers in the country. And cars cause acid rain, which is killing forests, rivers and streams and the wildlife that live in them. (You can find out more about acid rain in the next chapter.)

'I love the fresh air and the freedom to walk the streets safely. And although I love the freedom that a private car gives us, I know that with freedom comes responsibility and, unless we take a responsible view towards our environment, we may find it getting less and less beautiful. I once heard a phrase that I've always remembered: that we do not inherit the earth from our parents, but we borrow it from our children.'

Ben Elton, writer and comedian

Cars cost the earth

While motor vehicles are choking our towns and villages, road-building schemes are destroying the countryside. Over the last 30 years alone many important wildlife havens have been destroyed for road building. The Department of Transport got plenty of bad press recently when it bulldozed through the beautiful heathland of Snelsmore Common to build the Newbury Bypass. Anti-road activists made makeshift camps in the trees to protest against their destruction. Car enthusiasts in favour of the bypass cheered as the tree houses were toppled. But it wasn't just the road protesters that got the boot. Loads of endangered wildlife such as adders, dormice, kingfishers and rare bats were also left homeless as the road construction got under way.

During the 1980s and early 1990s the UK government had a policy to build new roads or enlarge existing ones to cope with increasing traffic. This motor madness encouraged even more cars onto the roads. Fortunately the last few years have seen a remarkable turn around in transport policy: the new Labour government has scrapped hundreds of road-building schemes the former government wanted to put in place. The government is planning to reduce road traffic, but not before time! In 1996 (the year before Labour came to power) 215 new cars hit the UK's streets every hour.

What does the public want?

A study carried out by the National Asthma Campaign in April 1994 showed that most people thought exhaust fumes should be reduced to protect children from asthma. One way in which car exhausts can be curbed is through catalytic convertors and since 1993 all new petrol (but not diesel) cars have had to be fitted with these.

Catalytic convertors (CATs) are supposed to cut emissions of some of the most harmful gases in car fumes by more than 75 per cent – or so their manufacturers would claim. In theory they are rarely so effective. Whatever, environmentalists agree that even a 75 per cent reduction is not enough to stop pollution reaching dangerous levels again, because car numbers are continuing to grow. And, more disturbingly, catalytic converters just haven't been built to last. When cars made in 1993 celebrated their third birthdays and went in for their first MOTs it was found that many of their CATs were already faulty, inefficient or completely broken.

Dirty diesel

If you think driving on diesel is safer than ordinary fuel, think again. Diesel fuel contains PM10s: particulates, or black sooty particles around 1/100th of a millimetre in size. These are so small that they can easily pass into your lungs and aggravate breathing problems. It's estimated that PM10s cause 8500 premature deaths every year in the UK. Diesel fuel also contains even finer PM2.5s. At 1/400th of a millimetre, they're about one quarter as small again as PM10s so they're even more dangerous. It has been proven that these particulates can kill and there is no safe level of this pollutant.

Curbing car use; why it's a political thing!

Friends of the Earth wants the government to crack down on unnecessary car use, especially on days when smogs occur. For despite the introduction of CATs to reduce traffic fumes, smogs are very much a fact of modern life; perhaps our most obvious evidence of air pollution.

FOE wants governments to introduce laws to get cars off the road. It believes that governments must set targets to reduce traffic levels. It's no good simply banning cars on certain days of the week for example. Mexico City drivers have had to obey an 'hoy no circula' (don't drive today) rule since 1990. Each vehicle is barred from driving on a certain day of the week, according to the last digit of the number plate. This campaign was designed to take one-fifth of the city's cars off the road on any given day. However, this isn't a foolproof way of curbing traffic. In some cases wealthy Mexico City residents simply wheel out their second or third cars, adding 300,000 vehicles to the road. Others simply switch number plates just to get around this rule!

FOE believes that national governments should set the framework for traffic reduction and that local authorities have a big role to play in reducing traffic in town centres and improving public transport. It believes that the public also has a big role to play, by responding to such measures by making a point of using its cars less, actually using public transport, and convincing other people to do so as well. A 5km car journey in a town or city emits 10 times as much carbon dioxide per passenger as a bus, and 25 times as much as a train.

Trains and buses use less energy, too. To transport one passenger 1km, a full car uses over four times as much energy as a full suburban electric train, and nearly seven times as much as a full double-decker bus.

The fuel and car industries have a significant role to play in pollution busting. For a start, the car industry is dependent on the fuel industry to a large degree, as it can't produce cars with reduced emissions and improved efficiency unless the fuel industry reduces the sulphur content of petrol and diesel.

The fuel industry has been forced by law to clean up its act, specifically to reduce the sulphur content of petrol and diesel. You may have seen low-sulphur fuels available at your local garage already. Changes have been agreed in Brussels that demand that fuel must be even cleaner by the year 2005.

> There are two main reasons why faster cars are more polluting than slower ones. Most car engines are designed to have their lowest fuel consumption at a steady 40 or 50mph. Also, from a pure physics point of view, it requires more energy to push a car forward at 70mph than it does at 50mph, so you burn more fuel and therefore produce more pollution.

There are, however, an awful lot of things the car industry can do to improve fuel consumption without changes to fuel. Technically it is possible to manufacture a small car that can travel 100 miles to the gallon, but there is little incentive because not enough people want to buy small cars. As long as the public wants to travel in flashy, powerful and spacious cars (which generally it does), with energy-draining add-ons such as stereos and air-conditioning systems, it will have less fuel-efficient vehicles. It's as simple as that! Car pollution can be curbed if everybody plays a part. When you think about buying a car, opt for a small, petrol-efficient car with a catalytic convertor.

Electric or hydrogen-powered cars are sometimes cited as pollution solutions. This is not necessarily the case, as electricity has to be generated and hydrogen manufactured and currently both these processes produce pollution. More importantly, such an alternative would not be practical. To date no electric or hydrogen-powered car exists that performs as well as a petrol or diesel car.

Governments can help by encouraging car drivers to drive smaller, fuel-efficient vehicles. At the moment, every car driver in the UK pays the same amount of road tax (to keep their vehicle on the roads) regardless of how polluting that vehicle is. By introducing different levels of road tax the government would encourage people to drive fuel-efficient cars. The government could also increase the duty payable on petrol and diesel to encourage people to use less fuel.

FOE also wants the government to encourage more companies to shift their goods by rail rather than road. In 1994, four and a half times the amount of goods were moved by lorries than in 1952. Industries use lorries and roads for distribution because they seem cheap compared with rail costs. However, road haulage would be far more expensive if it had to include the serious harm to the environment caused by heavy goods vehicles; a 38-tonne lorry passing over a piece of road causes as much damage as 100,000 cars.

Aeroplanes are a pain too...

Since the 1950s there has been a revolution in air traffic that has significantly contributed to global pollution. Air traffic has steadily increased to the point where 1200 planes take off from London's Heathrow airport every day – that's nearly one a minute! Planes guzzle gas and pump out fumes. People who live beneath flight paths aren't just bothered by noise; they get a slimy residue of pollution on their ponds too.

Flying by plane is often the only feasible way of getting from one country to another, but we can all reduce global air pollution by cutting down on the distances we travel by plane. A Boeing 747 flying from London to Bombay, for example, emits as much CO_2 as if each passenger had driven a car the same distance! The average distance driven by the average person in the UK in one year works out at about 6500 miles. But by taking just one long-haul flight per year we effectively double our contribution to the world's CO_2 overload.

Trains, like buses, are far less polluting per passenger because of the number of people they can carry. So, if you want to broaden your horizons with travel, consider inter-railing across Europe, or even further afield, rather than taking a long-haul flight to the Maldives.

Curbing the car

Cars are so much a part of modern life that it would be impractical and rather ridiculous to call for a return to a completely car-free society. Friends of the Earth is anti-traffic rather than anti-car. It recognises that cars and motor vehicles are a very useful and valuable part of modern life. Ambulances save lives by speeding the sick or injured to hospital. Buses take us to shop in (and out of) towns and cities. And cars carry us to work or to see friends who live miles away. Cars increase our independence and personal safety; car drivers can travel alone late at night without fear of personal attack, for example. Responsible car use can improve our quality of life – no doubt about it.

But sadly many of us have become 'car potatoes'. We use the car for short journeys that could easily be walked or cycled. FOE believes that if more people walked, cycled or travelled by bus or train, there would be millions fewer cars polluting our air each day, and that would mean a long-term improvement in air quality.

Industry could also help by coming up with more efficient vehicles but until they do Friends of the Earth recommends that we all curb our car use, leaving our cars at home at least two days a week and going by bike or bus, train or tram, or our own two feet instead.

It's time to pile on the pressure because cars are more than a cruel choke! Young people – yes, you! – are more car-dependent than any other generation in history. The amount of school-run traffic has more than doubled in the last twenty years, accounting for one in five of all rush-hour journeys. Today, less than one in ten students travel to school without adult supervision, mostly because of fear of traffic and accidents. The upshot of all this means that young people today have much less time hanging out with mates, having fun and most importantly, learning to be independent and self-reliant.

Five good reasons to curb the car...

1. If everyone pledged to leave their car at home just two days a week, there would be millions fewer cars polluting our air each day.
2. Cars use lots of energy. A full car uses around six times more energy per person than a full double-decker bus.
3. Fewer cars on the roads means fewer road accidents. At present over 4000 people are killed and 300,000 injured on our roads every year. Almost 40 per cent of 12- to 15-year-olds has a road accident travelling to school and most of these happen at the end of the school day.
4. Cycling is safer with fewer cars on the road. If there were fewer cars more cyclists would take to their bikes, which would then further reduce the amount of journeys made by car.
5. Walking, even short distances, is a great form of exercise. The British Heart Foundation recommends a brisk 20-minute walk every day to keep you fit and healthy.

...and three things governments must do to help

1. Make public transport cheaper, faster and more reliable and comfortable so more people actually prefer to use it. It's no wonder that we've all become so car-dependent when, over the last 20 years, rail fares have risen 75 per cent and bus fares by 60 per cent and yet overall motoring costs have fallen by nearly 7 per cent! Also, buses often get held up in traffic jams. Although there are priority bus lanes in most big cities, these aren't enforced as tightly as they could be. Freeing them from all other traffic would help whizz buses on their way.

2. Encourage rail use, particularly for long-distance travel and freight. Railways are cheaper to build and maintain than roads. Big lorries are a liability: they are up to eight times more likely than cars to be involved in fatal accidents. And one big lorry causes as much road damage as 100,000 cars!

3. Make cycling safer by setting up cycle lanes in every town and city. Cycling is much safer in countries such as Sweden, Holland and Germany, where there are good cycling facilities.

Pollution Busters!

Stop being part of the pollution problem – be part of the solution instead. There are lots of ways you can help curb the car and clean up our air. Read on and find out how.

Encouraging the government to act

Action on curbing the car must come from the government. So put pressure on it in one or more of these ways:

The government passed the Road Traffic Reduction Act in March 1997. This legally obliges local authorities to set targets for traffic reduction. You can help put pressure on them to act quickly. Write to your local council and ask what it is doing to reduce traffic in line with the new law.

Write to your local MP and ask her/him to put pressure on the government to make cleaner fuel cheaper. By the year 2005 all fuel sold in Europe must be much cleaner than it currently is. Reducing the cost now will increase demand for cleaner fuels and get fuel technology motoring!

Help put an end to road-building schemes altogether. Find out if there is an anti-road group near you, or whether there are any roads being built or widened in your area. Write to your local paper and council pointing out that new road schemes cause more traffic jams in the long run because they encourage more cars on to the roads. Start a petition to stop any unnecessary road schemes.

Campaign for traffic reduction in your area. Ask your friends to help you. Aim to each collect statements from 10 people confirming that they would leave their cars at home 2 days a week if public transport were better. Then present these statements to your local council. Invite the local press to photograph the presentation. Again, if you can give it a good picture opportunity it is more likely to turn up.

Start a petition to improve public transport and cycle facilities in your area. Demand better bus services, more cycle lanes and plenty of safe places to park your bike in town.

What you can do personally

Walk or cycle short journeys. Walking and cycling do virtually no damage to the environment. Cycling is actually quicker than all other alternatives to the car for journeys of less than five miles. Remember to wear a helmet and use proper lights, though, and it's safer to walk or cycle to school with a group of friends (single-file, of course!) – it's more fun, too.

Ask each member of your family to cut their car journeys. Car share whenever you can. Club together with your friends to set up a car-sharing scheme for the school run – if you can't get to school by any other means, of course! Car sharing reduces road traffic, saves petrol and gives parents more free time.

Invest in a travel pass. Ask your local education authority (or employer if you're working) for an interest-free travel-pass loan.

Lots of cyclists are put off biking because there are so few places to lock their cycles. If this is true for you, lobby your school, college or work to provide safe places to keep bikes and cycle helmets, and even to provide showering facilities.

Keen cyclists should ask their local education authority or employer for a loan towards a bike and a cycle-mileage travel allowance. The Body Shop, for example, offers employees the chance to buy bicycles at reduced rates.

Learn to become a responsible driver, not just a driver. That means being responsible not only about *when* you drive but *how* you drive. While out-of-town centres continue to spring up all around the country, driving is an essential skill for modern life. But learning to be an environmentally friendly driver is an even better skill!

Some steps to more eco-friendly driving
- if you are buying a car choose one that is fuel efficient
- a fast car is often highly polluting. Keep your speed down. Staying under 55mph where the national speed limit applies will help cut your polluting power
- do not tip oil, or other polluting materials, down the drain. Take your oil to a garage to be recycled
- make sure the car you drive runs on unleaded petrol.

Become a dirty diesel spotter! Keep a pad and pen with

you so you can report smoky diesel lorries, buses or coaches to the Vehicle Inspectorate Enforcement Group at your local Traffic Area Office. Make sure you take down the offending vehicle's licence-plate number and take a note of its make/model number and the date, time and place you saw it.

Seventeen-year-old Maria Coryell-Martin lives in the Laurelhurst district of Seattle, WA. She got the cycling bug 3 years ago when she bought her first bike and now regularly cycles 18 miles a day.

'When I got my first proper bike I was ecstatic! It was so good to have my very own independent transportation! I could go anywhere I wanted and have fun at the same time, I could spend time with my friends and stay in shape too. I spent that whole summer biking everywhere.

'I use my bike to cycle to school, to go rollerblading (or running) around a nearby lake and to visit friends. My parents were always against my biking to school because they were scared of me having an accident. But I found some friends who were willing to bike with me. Safety is something I always contemplate – and try to never compromise. I like biking anywhere I can as long as it's not really dark or raining cats and dogs.

'Not many people at my school cycle. It's either "I'm too lazy" or "It's too far!" etc. My school starts at 7.40 am so it is difficult for some to make the extra effort to bike. And I think most people just don't even consider it. Many would regard it as being too much trouble and are unaware of the benefits. But cycling makes you feel good. It's also so great when I've had a stressful day (especially at school) to push myself, to race through the hills and just exhaust myself. Then I always feel a little better.

'I wish people would become less dependent on cars.

I read in the news that America is becoming more and more overweight and that exercise is healthy. So why not bike? Besides lowering the number of cars on the road, bikes also help lower the levels of air pollution. (Smog is not only unhealthy, but gross.) I think the majority of the population would benefit from biking.

'We need to wean ourselves off environment-damaging habits. The earth is all we really have. This means being aware of our personal impact and acting. Recycling, practising a healthy lifestyle and protecting our environment should be things we do unconsciously. The ozone hole, smog and the depleting forests are all evidence that change needs to happen.

'Knowing that I cycle places that I could drive (and others do drive) makes me happy because I feel I am practising what I preach: staying healthy and being aware of the environment and our impact on it. The air we breathe in and the world we live in need to be a priority for all.'

Chapter 3
Polluted Waters

Fact: **In August 1998, 20 tonnes of a cancer-causing pollutant from a plastic PVC production plant leaked into Haifa Bay in northern Israel. Thousands of fish and other marine species were washed ashore dead.**

Fact: **In 1996 pollution levels on the shore of Homebush Bay, close to the site of Sydney's Olympic 2000 stadium, were found to be 380 times over the recommended 'safe limit'.**

Fact: **In 1993, 210 sewage works broke the law by over-polluting the rivers of England and Wales.**

Fact: **Persistent pollutants, such as PCBS and DDT, concentrating in the polar seas are causing declining birth rates in polar bears.**

Pure, fresh water: like fresh air, it's an essential for life. But just as our air is becoming choked, so our water supplies are being poisoned.

Everyday human activities are pumping pollution into different stages of the water cycle; from dumping sewage into the sea to pouring dangerous chemicals into our rivers. About one third of our tap water comes from water trapped under the ground. This 'groundwater', as it is called, is threatened by poisons leaking from rubbish dumps, farms and chemicals released into the environment by industry. Once polluted, groundwater is almost impossible to clean up.

In 1992 around 14 million people (about a quarter of all homes) in England and Wales drank polluted drinking water – by the way, boiling it doesn't help either! Unwittingly these people put not only their health but the chances of future generations at risk, because some experts believe that water pollution is affecting men's fertility. Recent research has shown that many men in the Thames Water area, which supplies London, have deformed sperm or low sperm counts. This may be due to the water they drink as the supply in much of London contains gender benders, which are known to make male fish develop female characteristics.

It is a criminal offence for a water company to supply water which is 'unfit for human consumption'. If you live in England and Wales and you notice brown, sludgy water coming out of your tap, contact the Drinking Water Inspectorate (see Hot Contacts! on page 142). It can prosecute water companies on behalf of consumers.

These days you'd have to be dying of thirst to take a sip of ordinary river water. Typically, rivers contain a disgusting cocktail of ingredients, including:
- farm waste, including animal excrement
- poisonous metals
- pesticides
- chemical effluents, including gender benders
- nitrates from fertilisers
- sewage.

Sewage effluent is the liquid discharged as 'waste' from sewage-treatment works. Raw or virtually raw ('preliminary treated') sewage is a dangerous pollutant on four accounts:

- effluent uses up oxygen as it breaks down, leaving less for the wildlife in rivers and oceans
- in hot summers, sewage pollution encourages algae to grow much faster. They bloom in vast numbers and can take up all the oxygen, suffocating fish and other water life. Sometimes the blooms are poisonous
- sewage contains bacteria and viruses. These can infect wounds and cause ear, nose and throat infections; stomach bugs; and eye, skin and chest infections, not to mention killer viral infections such as hepatitis and viral meningitis
- sewage treatment activates natural oestrogens excreted by women, causing gender benders. They've been found in the effluent from sewage-treatment works at high enough levels to feminise male fish.

Sewage-treatment works are one of the biggest polluters of Britain's rivers. A stretch of the River Lea downstream of the Luton Sewage Works is now 90 per cent sewage effluent. Sewage discharged into the UK's rivers and nine specially designated 'inland bathing waters' is given at least a 'secondary' treatment so that it is less polluting. This extra treatment uses bacteria and other small organisms to break down the sewage more (this is known as microfiltration) or uses ultraviolet light as a disinfectant. It doesn't kill all the viruses and bacteria contained in effluent but it does reduce the effluent's need for oxygen, leaving more for the fish and river animals to breathe. Sometimes, however, if the rain has been very heavy, the sewage system can overflow and cause pollution problems.

Surfing in sewage!

Staggeringly, every day 300 million gallons of raw or 'preliminary treated' sewage are pumped into the sea around the coast of Britain. That includes sanitary towels, tampons and panty-liners, since two billion of these are flushed down our toilets every year. In some coastal sites you can often spot a condom or two on the crest of a wave! Yet if all used towels and tampons were bagged and binned instead of flushed down the loo, they would make up only 0.03 per cent of household waste.

Eleven per cent of the population of England and Wales is serviced by a sewage-treatment works that only screens off solid matter.

Raw and preliminary treated sewage contain high levels of bacteria and viruses that can give swimmers and water sportsters ear, eye, skin and stomach infections. It is particularly dangerous because some of these – salmonella, for example – can remain active for over three months. In fact recent research has shown that UK surfers are three times more likely to catch hepatitis A than the general public. Surfers Against Sewage (SAS), a pressure group fighting against sea pollution, suggests that all surfers speak to their GP about getting a hepatitis A jab.

Sewage ending up on a beach isn't just risky to our health, it's also an eyesore and can be dangerous to wildlife, as animals can ingest it or get caught up in it. Five million sea birds and 100,000 marine animals including turtles and whales are estimated to die each year from swallowing plastic. Many plastics do not break down in the environment and therefore will remain there indefinitely. When tested for bacteria in the bathing water, one fifth of our beaches were below European standards. And at Porthtowan in Cornwall condoms, panty-liners and other sewage-related items are regularly washed up on the beach, despite the fact that the sewage outfall is supposed to be screened. But the UK doesn't have the dirtiest beaches in Europe by a long way. It's only halfway down the league table of other European countries. Greece and Spain are well ahead. Denmark and Germany have less clean bathing waters.

In the UK there are no rules limiting the types of waste that can be flushed down a toilet, although British sewers were not designed to deal with modern 'disposable' products. It has been estimated that nearly two thirds of all UK women flush away towels and tampons and one estimate suggests, not surprisingly, that 75 per cent of blocked drains are caused by sanitary products. In many countries people make a habit of bagging and/or binning all their sanitary waste to avoid blockages. And it is not unusual to see signs in homes, restaurants, hotels and offices politely asking people not to put sanitary products into the toilets.

So why the casual attitude in the UK? Chris Hines, general secretary and director of Surfers Against Sewage, explains: 'People in the UK put sanitary items down the toilet because of a lack of education. It is all too easy to flush and forget. Many people probably don't even give a second thought to where their rubbish might end up. People need to put two and two together and realise that what they flush down the toilet could end up bobbing along next to them when they go in the sea.' Chris, who describes his organisation as an 'experience-driven, solution-based campaign group that has taken the essence of surfing and applied it to politics and the environment,' goes on to say: 'Despite the UK having a marine heritage to be proud of, historically we have viewed the sea as a convenient sewer. For years there have been no votes in sewage. Now there are and we can make a difference.'

In the past water companies got up to all sorts of dirty tricks to bypass the EC's clean beach laws. One of these was to stop 'pumping and dumping' sewage into the sea during the holiday season. This had the effect of lowering scientific figures showing the bacterial and viral content of their waters, since these figures are averaged out over a whole year.

SAS argues that these companies should get with it and get real! Thanks to wetsuits, water sportsters now have fun in the sea all year round and hang about on the surf for many hours at a time. They are at risk of illness if the waters contain sewage effluent. Surfers Against Sewage believes that all sewage should be fully treated before being discharged. It also believes that the liquid and sludge content of treated sewage should be regarded as a resource, not as waste. In other words it wants an end to the 'pump and dump' approach to waste water in favour of 'clean up and recycle'.

And its big clean-up campaign is already having some success. A new EC Bathing Water Directive, which came into force in 1985, has set higher water (cleanliness) standards by reducing the acceptable levels of bacteria and viruses contained in bathing water near beaches. This directive has also set a level on inland bathing water – that's a first! – and is being policed by the Environment Agency. There has been a constant improvement in the quality of bathing water across Europe over the last few years. Water companies in the UK are currently spending millions of pounds improving sewage treatment. The Welsh Water Company, for example, is determined to keep to the new standards and win European Blue Flags for clean waters for its designated bathing beaches. It's an example that all water companies must follow.

As Chris Hines concludes: 'There is a very real, very practical solution to this problem. The technology is there, the experts are there. We should no longer be seeing sewage-polluted beaches or hearing about people that have become sick as a result of going in the sea.'

Dangerous chemicals awash in our water!

There are thousands of pollutants that have worked their way into the water cycle. Some of them have already been mentioned since they are present in the air (and as a result affect our water supply). Here are a few more of the most common.

Pollutant: NITRATES (artificial fertilisers)
How they pollute our water supplies: nitrates enter the water cycle when they are sprayed on farm land to boost crops. Fertilisers get washed into the soil, where they sink down further into the water-table. Rain also washes nitrates into streams and rivers from which water companies draw our water supplies. There are often illegal levels of nitrates in drinking water.

They can make us ill because they may cause stomach (gastric) cancer and 'blue baby' syndrome, a blood disorder. A recent study at Leeds University for Health

Services Research discovered a link between nitrates and diabetes in children under 16.

Pollutant: PESTICIDES

How they pollute our water supplies: they enter the water cycle when they are sprayed on (non-organic) farm land to protect crops from pests and fungi. Like fertilisers, they get washed into rivers or deep down into the soil.

They can make us ill because, although they may not be harmful at low levels, pesticides can build up in plants and in the animals that feed on them. Animals at the top of the food-chain, such as herons and otters, can accumulate very high levels of pesticides in their bodies, which can stop them breeding. (There's more about this in chapter four.)

In recent years more than 43 different pesticides have been found in this country's drinking water at illegally high levels. The good news is that new EC laws mean that water companies are having to install treatment plants to remove pesticides. The bad news is that the cost of such plants is an estimated £800 million, and it'll be the customer that foots the bill!

Pollutant: HERBICIDES

How they pollute our water supplies: in the same way as pesticides, mentioned above, when they are sprayed on crops to stop weeds growing.

They can make us ill because, like pesticides, herbicides build up in plants and in the animals that feed on them and harm animals at the top of the food-chain. Using fewer chemicals for farming would cut river pollution and would also mean fewer problems for wildlife. Atrazine and simazine are the two herbicides most commonly found in Britain's drinking water and were widely used as weedkillers by local authorities. A study of births in Iowa, US found that mothers who drank water contaminated with herbicides such as atrazine were more likely to have babies that grew less in the womb. Thanks to Friends of the Earth's campaigning, all non-agricultural uses of atrazine and simazine are now banned.

Modern pesticides and herbicides work so well because they remain active long after they've been sprayed. But unfortunately this also makes them the perfect pollutants. Isoproturon, a weedkiller used in the Thames Valley, stays in the environment and ends up contaminating London's drinking water. In 1992 in the UK's Thames region, 144 supply zones, serving some 4.6 million people, contained isoproturon in excess of EC standards.

Pollutant: PHOSPHATES

How they pollute our water supplies: they are included in laundry detergents to soften water, which helps improve cleaning power. Between 20 and 60 per cent of the phosphates present in Britain's waters is derived from detergents. The rest comes from agriculture and human waste.

They can make us ill because too much can cause algae blooms, killing off other plant life and animal life. Some (but not all) algae blooms can be toxic and cause pneumonia, stomach bugs, skin and eye irritations, sickness and headaches in humans.

Pollutant: LEAD

Where it comes from: lead supply pipes in the home.

It can make us ill because it can affect the central nervous system and brain functions. And most worryingly it can retard young children's intellectual development. Your water company may not be able to tell you whether or not your tap water is affected. But you can look yourself, or get a plumber to check. Lead pipes are softer, so they have less regular shapes than copper or steel pipes. If you have got lead pipes some protection from lead can be achieved by running the tap for a few minutes before using the water for drinking or cooking. This isn't ideal, of course, because it wastes water. Contact the Environmental Health Officer at your local council for more advice.

Pollutant: OIL

Where it comes from: oil can be washed into our drinking water from petrol filling stations and storage tanks or by being poured down our drains. It can also enter the water cycle from sea-based refineries but more significantly from spills at sea. Enough crude oil to fill about 1154 Olympic-sized swimming pools has been spilled at sea since 1975. Oil accounts for one quarter of all pollution incidents in the UK or over 6000 oil-pollution incidents each year.

It is dangerous because it forms a film on the surface of rivers and lakes, drastically reducing the level of oxygen in the water and making it difficult for fish to breathe. It can also coat plants and animals that come into contact with it. Oil spills cause havoc on our coastlines and beautiful beaches and devastate birds and marine life.

In 1996 the oil tanker *Sea Empress* ran aground off the coast of south west Wales and created the UK's worst single oil spill. Despite a massive clean-up operation, lichens and mosses have disappeared from many rocks. These are at bottom of the food-chain, which means that many animals there must be starving.

Pollutant: INDUSTRIAL CHEMICALS

Where they come from: from industry! Thousands of different types of chemicals get discharged into rivers from factories, or simply poured on the ground, where they seep down to pollute underground water supplies. While you would almost certainly be fined under local by-laws if you were caught littering, a large factory is often allowed to release an agreed amount of toxic waste into water (and land and air). Amazing, eh?

They can make us ill because many of these can accumulate in body fat. This can cause long-term damage to the immune and reproduction systems.

If this list makes things sound bad – and they are (there were over 25,000 proven water-pollution incidents in England and Wales in 1993 alone) – listen to this: water pollution is being made worse by the very companies who supply us with pure, clean water. This is because in 1989 the government privatised the Water Board and gave regional water companies the right to drain water from rivers. As a result the British water industry is legally allowed to run our rivers dry. And the less water rivers contain, the more concentrated any pollution becomes. Llyn Tegrid is the largest natural lake in Wales. It has been designated a site of Special Scientific Interest and is home to rare species such as the floating water plantain and the glutinous snail. Yet to meet future water demands there is a proposal to pump water from the lake.

We need to cut down on the amount of water we use so that we can protect our rivers and streams without needing to build expensive reservoirs. Friends of the Earth believes that we should aim for a 15 per cent reduction in the amount of water we take from the environment. Your water company should take steps to save water itself (it is thought that around one quarter of water is lost through leaks in water company pipes). It should also help you to save water. Write to it (its address is on your water bill) and ask it for water-saving ideas to add to the ones at the end of this chapter.

Acid rain

Acid rain is one form of pollution most of us are familiar with, since it has had a lot of press – all of it bad! Acid rain is water that has been over-acidified by pollution in the air. And it's a prime example of just how delicate the earth's ecosystem is. Acid rain is formed when air pollution mixes with water vapour in the atmosphere.

Acid rain is an international problem and, until we can make clouds stay exactly within our own countries (not very likely!), it needs an international effort to tackle the problem. Actually acid rain is a misleading term that plays down the seriousness of the problem. Think air pollution meets water pollution and you get acid snow, acid hail and acid fog, not to mention acid mist, acid drizzle and acid slush – all of which are harmful to the environment.

If you opted out of science at school, here's a crash

course in the chemistry of acids and alkalines, which should give you an understanding of the issue. Acidity and its opposite, alkalinity, are measured on the pH scale, which runs from 1 to 14:

- pH 1 is very acid
- pH 7 is neutral
- pH 14 is very alkaline.

Normal rain is only slightly acidic: about pH 5.6. But when mixed with polluting gases such as sulphur dioxide (SO_2) and nitrogen dioxide (NO_2), rain becomes too acidic. These days most UK rainfall is affected; it averages between pH 4.2 and 4.8.

It's already been pointed out that acid rain is crumbling our oldest architectural treasures and that it's falling into rivers, lakes and streams, killing the fish and plants that live there. Many lakes in Norway and Sweden, covering thousands of square kilometres, are now technically 'dead' (no life is growing there any more) — or at least severely damaged — as a result of acid rain. Much of this blew across the sea from the UK (which produces more sulphur dioxide than any other EC country).

The UK is having its own problems with acid rain. UK trees are showing symptoms of leaf loss, which are among the worst in Europe; nearly one in four of our trees are affected. And increasing acidity of rivers and lakes is killing our marine wildlife, particularly affecting the breeding cycles of frogs and the rare natterjack toad.

But the effects of acid rain go far beyond harming one or two species; the combination of changes in the forests, soils, lakes and rivers is affecting the way these ecosystems work together. From dog whelks turning male because of the killer chemicals painted on ships hulls (to stop molluscs building up on them) to reproduction problems in all kinds of wildlife and perhaps humans, governments all around the world must wise up pretty sharpish because there's simply no time to waste!

Pollution Busters!

Water pollution is something no one should have to swallow. There's lots you can do about it.

What you can do personally

Save water. Our demand for water is so great these days that water companies are draining rivers to cope. The less water rivers contain, the more concentrated any pollution becomes. Each of us uses about 140 litres of water per day per household. A bath uses 80 litres of water, while a shower uses around 40 litres on average. So take showers instead of baths.

Most toilets in Britain use 10 litres of water per flush. Newer low-flush toilets use between 5 and 8 litres. By getting a low-flush toilet you could cut your household's water use by 10 per cent. Alternatively you could fit a special 'water hippo' (brick in a bag) available from your local water company into your cistern to save water. Having a low-water washing machine would cut up to 30 per cent – while giving you the same quality wash you get with wasteful regular machines. Tell your parents to look out for the 'EC Ecolabel', which indicates low-water toilets and household washing machines.

Slap a hosepipe ban on your household. The average rooftop receives 40,000 litres of water per year as rain. This could be caught in water butts and used to water the garden instead of hosepipes.

Wash your clothes less frequently! Not that you want to be grotty, but you really don't need to wash that pair of jeans when you've only worn them once. Very often clothes don't need washing; they just need to be brushed clean and aired to freshen them up. Plus, it will make your clothes last longer. When you do use your washing machine use less detergent than recommended.

Go organic! Support organic farmers by buying (or asking whoever is in charge of the weekly shop in your household to buy) as many organic foods as possible. Non-organic produce is priced lower but this doesn't reflect the true cost to the environment.

Rubbish dumps sometimes cause water-pollution problems, so make sure you reuse and recycle as much as you can.

Bag and bin your tampons and sanitary towels, especially if you live in an area where sewage is pumped raw or virtually untreated out to sea, as this will help decrease the amount of bacteria and viruses present in your local sea water.

Never chuck household chemicals (such as oil, turps and paint remover) down the drain. Get rid of them at your nearest tip. Phone your council to find out where this is or contact Waste Watch, a UK-based charity who advocate waste reduction, reuse and recycling (see Hot Contacts! on page 147).

Write to the Environment Agency and ask for information about local companies and farmers who are legally polluting rivers and streams in your area. You can mail these companies and alert them to the problems they're causing locally and further afield through their actions. Ask them when they're going to clean up their acts!

Is bottled any better?

Some people buy bottled water because they think this is better for them than drinking tap water. Bottled water uses a lot of energy in the bottling and distribution process, which causes pollution. Another downside of drinking bottled water is that most of it comes in plastic containers. In theory these are recyclable; in practice only 1 per cent ever actually are!

Drinking tap water is better for the environment. But if you want to drink bottled water:

- make sure you choose a variety that doesn't have to be shipped halfway across the world to get to you
- buy it in glass bottles if possible and take your empties to a bottle bank. If you must buy plastic bottles then make sure you recycle these, too.
- choose bottled water explicitly labelled 'natural mineral water'. Water flagged up as 'mineral water', 'spring water', 'spa water' or 'table water' is drawn from rivers and reservoirs and so could just as well have come from your taps.

If you're worried about the quality of tap water, persuade your parents to buy a water filter. These remove chemical traces and improve taste. This is an expensive option, however, because filters need to be replaced regularly.

If you live near a river or stream keep an eye out for river pollution and algae blooms. Report all signs of river pollution to the pollution police. Your local environment agency officers need your help in spotting the first signs of pollution so that they can act quickly to track down the polluters and make them pay. Phone the Environment Agency (see Hot Contacts! on page 142–143) if you spot scum, dead fish and/or smelly/odd-coloured water. Calls are free.

Find out what's in your drinking water. You won't need wellies or jam-jars because water companies do thousands of tests each year for particular chemicals and micro-organisms in the water they supply. The results are kept on a public register kept by the company itself. It can also give you a list of the legal standards for comparison and can tell you how many times it has found individual pollutants or groups of pollutants at levels above legal limits.

If you find your drinking water exceeds the legal standards for water consumption, you can kick up a fuss! Write back to your water company and ask how much money it is spending on taking pollution out of drinking water and whether the polluters are contributing to the cost.

If you're a water-sports fan, write to the Environment Agency and ask it how clean your nearest windsurfing or sailing lake's water is.

Encouraging the government to act

Write to the prime minister. Ask for tougher laws preventing industry and farms from dumping dangerous toxins in rivers. Rivers, lakes and underground water should be protected from pollution by severely restricting the use of pesticides, nitrate fertilisers and industrial chemicals (especially gender benders, which threaten the future of humankind!) in areas where they might do damage. And ask for tougher punishments for those that break the law.

Write to your local MP, asking her/him to campaign for tighter controls on sewage dumping. Even if you're not big on riding those waves, think about supporting Surfers Against Sewage because of their enlightened work on cleaning up our coastal waters.

Seventeen-year-old Nicola Bunt lives in St Agnes, Cornwall on Britain's south west coast. She has been surfing since she was 14 and now surfs competitively. Nicola often spends up to four hours a day in the sea where she is at risk from high levels of pollution.

'I worry about pollution and getting ill. There is a sewage outfall just around the headland at St Agnes but fortunately the treatment plant now includes UV treatment, which significantly reduces the bacteria and virus levels in the water. Supposedly it's safe to surf here without the risk of infection, though in reality there have been one or two problems from time to time, which means the pathogens aren't removed. You can tell when this happens because the water is a dirtier brown colour and scummy.

'Sometimes I surf at nearby Porthtowan, where the waves are bigger and more powerful. I've seen raw sewage in the water there, and tampons, condoms, needles and plastic strips often get washed up on the beach. The sea smells worse and the water is browner. But it's the invisible viruses and bacteria that worry me most, because when I'm surfing I tend to swallow a lot of water. A lot of it goes up my nose and in my ears, too.

'My dad and I went surfing together once and we both came down with a stomach bug. Generally speaking I've been lucky, though, with my health. A friend of mine recently had an ear operation because of all the infections he'd picked up from the sea.

'I decided to join Surfers Against Sewage because I want to stop sewage being dumped into our seas. The problem is pretty bad right now and I don't want it to get worse. SAS are doing something about it and I'm proud to put their stickers all over my board.

'It's time we stopped using our seas as sewers and started protecting them for future generations. If I had a daughter I'd be worried about her surfing. I'm not sure if I would encourage her to spend as much time as I do in the sea, though I'm hopeful that things will change.'

Chapter 4

More Toxic Shocks

Fact: **About one third of the PCBS (persistent hormone disruptors) ever produced are still in the environment.**

Fact: **In 1998 alone, 14,315 tonnes of cancer-causing chemicals, 1,640,483 tonnes of acid-rain gases and 100,951 mgs of dioxins, were pumped out into the atmosphere by Britian's factories.**

Fact: **New research has shown that chemicals added to the plastics in many phones, TVS and computers can permanently damage the brains of mice.**

Fact: **Over six million electrical goods are dumped every year in the UK, contributing to the 'toxic time-bomb' effect of our landfill sites.**

Persistent chemicals: here today, here tomorrow

As you'll have realised from reading the last chapter, industrial chemicals are major players in environmental pollution. This chapter focuses on industry's most deadly suspects: persistent chemicals.

Persistent chemicals are particularly toxic because they don't break down in the environment or in our bodies.

Instead they build up, even when they are no longer being used. Some persistent chemicals are very soluble in fats; they accumulate in the body fat of fish, animals and humans. Certain chemicals pollute entire food–chains. Hundreds of chemical contaminants including dioxins are found in fish oils, dairy products, human fat and breast milk. In fact, eating animal fat is the major source of dioxins for humans.

Chemical build up in breast milk: breast-feeding is still best

Most human breast milk contains traces of pollutants (usually absorbed during the previous 10 years). But breast-feeding is still by far the best option for babies. And it's the most environmentally friendly way to feed a baby, too. For a start it doesn't require plastic bottles that need to be sterilised with chemicals or earth-costly electricity. Available on tap and for free, it strengthens babies' resistance to infection and protects them against any infections the mother is exposed to. Research suggests that breast-fed babies have a reduced risk of chest infections, urinary tract infections, eczema and diabetes and may well be more intelligent with better nervous-system development than bottle-fed babies. If you breast-feed you'll benefit, too, getting protection against pre-menopausal breast cancer, ovarian cancer and hip fractures in old age.

Even withstanding its dioxin content, breast milk is a better option because formula milk contains pollutants that we don't even know about. And the good news is that levels of dioxin in breast milk in the UK fell by about 35 per cent between 1988 and 1994, largely because of improved pollution control; proof that cleaning up the environment can make a real difference to human health.

We are also exposed to persistent pollutants by inhaling them, after they've been sprayed in our homes or after they've evaporated into the air from household products (from carpets and computer equipment, for example). In other words, these chemicals work their way into our bodies in many ways.

Children are more susceptible to pollution than adults because:

- many parts of their bodies are developing (particularly their brains and reproductive organs), which means they are more susceptible to alterations
- their bodies can't break down chemicals as well as an adult body can
- they eat, drink and breathe more for their weight than adults and so take in relatively more contaminants
- they tend to be breathing air closer to the ground, which may contain more dust than that higher up.

Gender benders (as hormone disruptors are generally known), such as dioxins, have been briefly mentioned earlier in this book. Along with PCBs, which we'll get to soon, they are a very serious form of pollution because we don't yet know the full impact they have on us and other animals.

Hormones are substances that carry a message around the body through the blood. When a hormone reaches the right destination its message is put into action. Our bodies produce more than 50 different hormones (or chemical messengers) that influence many aspects of the body. They regulate our metabolism and affect sexual characteristics. Gender benders or hormone disrupting chemicals are able to play tricks on our bodies by imitating, or disrupting, the action of natural hormones. The female hormone oestrogen, the male hormone testosterone and the thyroid hormones seem particularly vulnerable to gender benders.

As well as being linked with testicular, breast and prostate cancer, gender benders may be responsible for a recent decline in men's sperm counts. And as a Friends of the Earth's Industry and Pollution Campaigner puts it: 'Diminished sperm count is a serious matter. Many animals produce up to 1400 times as much sperm as is needed for fertility. In contrast, the average human male produces only two to four times as much as is needed for fertility – they don't have much sperm to spare. A 50 per cent reduction in human sperm count may make significant numbers of males infertile.'

The growth and development of our bodies as we grow up is controlled by hormones. Hormones are particularly crucial when a baby is developing in its mother's womb and in early childhood, as their signals control developing reproductive organs, and the growth and development of the brain. That's why babies in the womb are so sensitive to toxic chemicals and can be damaged by them.

Gender benders have been linked with problems in the development of the reproductive organs. We don't know much about the potential impact they may have on our intelligence and behaviour.

Some plants such as soya contain natural chemicals that disrupt hormones – gender bend – but the human body can break them down rapidly because we have been exposed to plant hormones throughout our evolution.

The following chemicals have been included in this chapter for one reason: they are either persistent or gender bending, or both. In short, they mean trouble!

The first three chemicals mentioned here are being phased out. However, they are still a danger because even though they are not being manufactured they remain in the environment and our bodies. There's nothing we can do to remove persistent chemicals from the planet once they've been released.

Pollutant: PCBS (or polychlorinated biphenyls)

Where they come from: they originally evaporate into the air and leach into our water from printing inks, paints, plasticisers and some electrical parts. During the 1960s PCBs were recognised as a major environmental pollutant. It became clear then that PCBs are extremely persistent and build up in animal or human fat. Since then they have contaminated our food supplies and so have worked their way around the world. They are found in human fat and breast milk, with particularly high levels at the North and South Poles, where they are taken by prevailing winds, cold water currents and weather patterns. Some polar bears, whales and seals living in the polar regions have been found with enough chemicals accumulated in their fat that scientists have on occasion declared them 'toxic waste'.

Because they are gender benders: they can affect fertility and sexual behaviour. Water creatures such as otters and herons are becoming infertile from the effects of PCBs building up in their bodies. Otters have disappeared from six rivers in East Anglia because of this problem. On the more positive side, PCBs are no longer produced in Europe and many nations have agreed to stop producing them and to try to destroy those in use before they start polluting the environment.

Pollutant: DDT (dichlorodiphenyltrichloroethane)

Where it comes from: pesticides, particularly for mosquito control but also in general farming. Once DDT was used all over the world; now it is mainly used in the majority world. Our bodies turn DDT into DDE and both of these compounds stick around in the human body and the environment.

Because it is a gender benders: it is dangerous. One form of DDE has been proven to block the action of the male hormone androgen in mice.

Research is suggesting that girls in the US are now going through puberty earlier than has been found in past studies. This is thought to be because their mothers had high levels of PCBs and DDEs in their bodies while they were pregnant. Girls whose mothers had the highest levels, and who were therefore exposed to the highest amounts of DDEs and PCBs in the womb, entered puberty almost a year (11 months) earlier than girls with lower exposures.

Pollutant: PCTS (polychlorinated terphenyls)

Where they come from: they were used in electrical components. They are no longer in use (production of these chemicals stopped in the late 1970s) but, as you've probably suspected, these persistent polluters are still with us; they've been found in human blood and fat. There's no known way of removing them from our environment.

Because they are gender benders: they may cause fertility problems. They may cause cancers, too.

Pollutant: APES (alkylphenol ethoxylates or alkylphenols)

Where they come from: they are used in industrial and agricultural detergents. There are also a range of other alkylphenol derivatives in industrial use; for example, in some plastic products.

Because they are gender benders: they mimic oestrogen, causing the development of female characteristics in males. They've been shown to affect wildlife even at very low concentrations.

Pollutant: DIOXINS

Where they come from: minute traces of dioxins may have existed before industrialisation but a huge rise occurred, starting in the 1940s. As already mentioned in chapter one, these get released into the air when chlorine-containing materials, such as most sanitary towels and tampons, are incinerated. Eating animal fat is the major source of exposure to dioxins for humans.

Because they are gender benders: they are dangerous. Dioxins are suspected of causing reduced sperm counts, reduced fertility, genital malformations and endometriosis (where the lining of the womb starts to grow in other parts of the abdomen. It can cause painful periods and fertility problems). They are one of the most dangerous persistent pollutants on earth. Even at very low levels they can cause cancer and have been linked to learning difficulties, as well.

Chlorine is used to bleach wood pulp to make white paper. During this process dioxins are formed. Paper mills then discharge dioxin-polluted effluent into our rivers. Chlorine is not used in wood pulping in Britain but chlorine-bleached pulp is imported and so supports the continuation of an extremely polluting process in other countries. You can do your bit to stamp it out by only buying paper products (including tampons and sanitary towels) made from unbleached and non-chlorine bleached pulp – without plastic liners or applicators too. If you're in doubt about whether a product is made from unbleached and non-chlorine bleached pulp just look on the box. Manufacturers always shout out about the environmentally friendly aspects of their products whenever they can!

Pollutant: BRFS (brominated flame retardants; a group of chemicals)

Where they come from: they are contained in many products such as carpets and computer equipment to make them more fire-resistant. BRFs evaporate into the air from such products or get released into the environment during their manufacture.

Because they are gender benders: they are dangerous. They are so persistent they have even worked their way into the blubber of sperm whales in the remote deep waters of the Atlantic. When burnt, materials containing BRFs can emit dioxin-like chemicals. In Sweden levels of one BRF, called polybrominated diphenyl ether (PBDE for short), found in human breast milk have increased by 50 times over the past 25 years. High levels of PDBEs have also been discovered in the blood of workers at an electronics-dismantling plant.

Pollutant: MUSK SCENTS

Where they come from: scented products including toilet cleaners, shaving foam, washing-up liquid, make-up and perfumes. Artificial musks are persistent and build up in animal and human fat.

Why they are dangerous: they contaminate the wider

environment, including fish, and accumulate in our bodies, contaminating human fat, blood and breast milk. It's almost impossible to detect (and therefore avoid) products that contain musk scents since the ingredients are not always listed on the packaging. So choose natural essential oils instead of perfume and avoid scented products in general wherever you can.

Pollutant: PHTHALATES

Where they come from: plastic products (they are used to make plastics more flexible and are found in lots of teethers and soft toys).

Why they are dangerous: phthalates don't stick around in the same way as persistent chemicals do but they are still dangerous because many are gender benders. Research has shown that these plasticisers leak out into food and drink and can also leach out of the toys into the mouths of children chewing them! Austria has banned the use of phthalates in toys for children under three.

Pollutant: BPA (bisphenol a.)

Where it comes from: it is used to make protective coatings inside many (but not all) tin cans, where it can leach into our food.

Because it is a gender bender: it can affect our fertility.

In the 20th century we have experienced, literally, a revolution in the production and use of chemicals. Since World War Two our bodies and the environment have been exposed to many new chemicals. Around 100,000 different chemicals were in use in the EU in 1981 and yet the vast majority of these have not been adequately tested for safety. Although there are now stricter international agreements in place concerning chemicals, both new and old, we still know very little about the effects they can have on our health when they are combined. And yet every day we are exposed to mixtures of chemicals rather than just any one chemical.

What is perhaps more worrying is that even though safe levels have been established concerning chemical pollutants, scientists haven't taken into account the fact that there is no such thing as the norm! Different people's bodies are affected differently by polluting chemicals. Some of us can't break down chemicals as easily as others can and so are more susceptible to their effects. But the current safety levels for chemicals are generally set by considering a 'normal' member of the population rather than the most sensitive people.

If you've read this far you've probably come to the conclusion that industry has a lot to answer for. The truth is that industry really needs to clean up its act. Clean technology makes good economic – as well as environmental – sense. It wastes less resources and raw materials. Technology that would reduce waste and cause less pollution is available. The chemical industry must stop manufacturing persistent chemicals and develop safer alternatives: they have a responsibility to protect human health and the environment.

Pollution Busters!

Follow these measures and cut down on your chemical consumption.

What you can do personally

Be committed to using less chemicals!

- don't use perfumes; use essentials oils instead. These are extracted from plants and so are biodegradable

- forget chemical air fresheners. Burn essential oils instead. Or if you don't have a burner you can perfume a room by adding a few drops of essential oil to a bowl of warm water left on your radiator

- don't use a deodorant/antiperspirant. You won't smell as long as you wash under your arms every day and shower after sport. Sweat doesn't smell unless it becomes stale on the skin. Look for natural deodorants that contain only essential oils as perfumes, available from health stores. Or why not try the deodorant stone instead. It's a block of stone that you simply rub on your skin. Perfume-free, it's claimed to be very effective!

- don't buy make-up or cleaning products containing nonoxynol or nonylphenol ethoxylate (gender bending chemicals) or products made of PVC

- don't buy clothes that need dry-cleaning. Dry-cleaning fluids contain highly polluting chemicals

- use water-based paints.

Alert your family or flatmates to the toxic dangers that could be lurking in your home.

You can reduce your intake of dioxin-like chemicals by going vegan or veggie. Read *The Livewire Guide to Going, Being and Staying Veggie!* by Juliet Gellatley.

Or, if you don't want to give up meat, buy organic food where possible; that's food grown without the use of artificial fertilisers, herbicides and pesticides. It's better for our health and it's better for the planet. There's more about organic farming in chapter six.

Encouraging the government to act

Write to the Minister for Environment or your MP and express your concern about your right to know what is in all products. Ask the government to publish a comprehensive list of pollutants that will inform people about local sources of pollution. Also request that the government sets up health studies to determine the effects of landfill sites, factories and other sources of pollution on our health.

Write to your MP and demand that all persistent or bioaccumaltive chemicals be phased out. FOE believes that all synthetic chemicals in use should break down rapidly into harmless, natural substances. There should be no accumulation in the human body, wildlife or the environment, unless this is an essential function of a chemical used for a very special purpose.

Chapter 5
Rubbishing Our Land

Fact: **In the US rubbish dumps (or landfill sites, as they are often called) are being dug up to reclaim recyclables and create more space for more rubbish!**

Fact: **Each year in the UK we use 6000 million glass bottles and jars. That's one every day in every household. Most just get thrown away.**

Fact: **Before the mid-1970s, very few records were kept of what went into the UK's landfill sites, so many older sites contain unknown quantities of toxic chemicals.**

Fact: **A recent European study found that the babies born to women living near hazardous waste dumps were a third more likely to have birth defects than those born to mothers living further away.**

The world and its population of greedy consumers is piling up mountains of so-called waste. In the US, wood and paper thrown away each year is enough to heat five million homes for 200 years. And in the UK alone, every year we throw away 26 million tonnes of household rubbish; that's nearly one tonne for each home or about 90 dustbins full. But when rubbish is thrown out it doesn't really 'go away'. It just goes somewhere else where it becomes a pollution problem!

Dumping waste in the ground doesn't make sense. It's practically impossible to keep waste products exactly where you leave them. Inevitably, that waste or parts of it will find its way into the environment.

In the UK most household rubbish ends up in landfill sites. There it rots down, generating methane gas and noxious liquids. As it rots, harmful liquids can leak out and pollute rivers and groundwater. Rain seeps through to buried waste and produces a liquid called 'leachate', which can also contaminate rivers and underground water reserves. Hundreds of UK landfill sites pose a serious risk of polluting water and many are already leaking. Landfill sites built by the Romans some 2000 years ago are still producing leachate!

Farm pollution and industrial pollution in the UK, has already forced some underground water-holes to be closed. On the other side of the globe, pollution from the Ok Tedi copper and gold mine in New Guinea has contaminated local seafood. This is now considered to have destroyed the ecosystem on which 30,000 people depended for their livelihoods.

Rotting organic waste produces methane gas. If this builds up underground it can cause explosions. Three people were seriously injured in Derbyshire in 1986 when gas from a closed tip built up and exploded in a bungalow nearby. A government survey into this problem found that 1390 open or recently closed landfill sites were gassing or potentially gassing. Literally, they're ready to blow!

Up in smoke

At present about 5 per cent of the UK's rubbish gets incinerated or burnt rather than buried. This is particularly polluting, as it puts out dioxins, heavy metals, dust, particles and acid gases into the air, which (as you'll know from the previous chapters) can all seriously damage our health. And what happens to the toxic ashes that incineration always leaves? Yes, you guessed it, they end up being buried, and so they are more likely to pollute our groundwater than unburnt waste.

Currently the UK government plans to burn more waste from households, shops and offices. Many of the new proposed incinerators will be able to generate electricity from the heat produced by waste burning. And some of them will use the heat directly to heat buildings. For this reason the government isn't calling them incinerators (a word that most people associate with pollution). Instead they've been given a new name: 'waste-to-energy' or 'energy-from-waste' facilities.

Friends of the Earth believes that neither burning waste nor burying it is the answer because of the pollution problems they both cause.

Reduce, reuse, recycle

Chucking out mountains of trash each year doesn't just create serious pollution problems. It also puts a huge demand on the earth's precious resources. It's reckoned that ten tonnes of resources are used to make just one tonne of 'product'. And everything we use has to come from somewhere. Wildlife habitats are damaged and pollution caused when resources are mined, harvested and refined to make everyday products such as newspapers and cans. That's why reducing our waste, and reusing or recycling goods – is the only way to stop the rot.

There's no point in chucking things out if they can be

repaired. More containers could be made in standardised shapes and sizes so they can be reused many times over. Washing and refilling a container often takes less energy than making a new one, whether from raw materials or those collected for recycling.

If waste can't be reused or repaired then recycling is the answer. Recycling means using the same materials again and again – materials that would otherwise be wasted. Many products can be recycled by breaking them down to make new ones. Recycling is also important because it helps to stop littering. It has helped clean up the streets in many North American cities. Recycling shows people that tins, bottles and scraps of paper have a value. That makes people less likely to drop them on the ground.

Almost 80 per cent of our rubbish could be recycled but only around 7 per cent actually is. The UK government set a target of 25 per cent by the year 2000; a target it did not meet, because not enough local authorities didn't (and still don't) run door-to-door collections. Some councils did, of course (and still do), and have been setting high standards for recycling that are positively encouraging. The London Borough of Sutton, for example, plans to recycle 80 per cent of household waste by 2006. If every council in the UK achieved just half of that recycling rate – say 40 per cent, as has been done in parts of the US – it would create up to 12,000 new jobs.

Even if your local council does collect waste for recycling you may be being misled. Collecting waste for recycling is only one step in a cycle. It must then be reprocessed and used. By law, councils should have to recycle a certain amount of each type of material. And to complete the cycle, it's important to buy products made from recycled products!

Talking rubbish bins – all going to waste!

Let's take a closer look at some of the valuable resources we're binning and how these could be better disposed of.

Paper

If the annual total quantity of the UK's printing and writing paper was stacked onto an average-sized football pitch, the resulting column would be about as high as Telecom Tower. One year's worth of the paper used in British newspapers alone would wrap around the equator 270 times.

Paper makes up about a third of all household waste, mostly from newspapers and magazines and packaging. And yet only a third of the paper we use in the UK gets recycled. We're literally dumping the world's forests into our waste bins: five million tonnes of paper and 500,000 tonnes of wood is being landfilled every year!

About one third of the rubbish in the average dustbin is discarded packaging. Out of every £75 spent on groceries, £10 is for the packaging. If this is something that you've never given much consideration before, dive in head first and unwrap a week's shopping in one go. Look at each item in turn and think about how it is packaged. Does it have more than one layer of packaging? Can it be refilled? Can it be reused? Is it made of recycled materials? Can you recycle it, or parts of it, in your local area? Chances are that

'Yes' won't figure too highly in your answers, more's the pity. It's a problem that we all can tackle as consumers but that governments must act on, too. For example, in Germany overpackaging has been reduced by a law that makes industry responsible for recycling its waste. It means that shoppers leave excess wrapping at the supermarket to be returned to the producer. This is something that the rest of the world should be doing.

More paper-recycling schemes are needed, and the market for recycled paper needs to increase too. Currently British newspapers use less than 50 per cent recycled fibre – they could use more. And a far greater proportion of products such as toilet tissue could be made from 100 per cent recycled paper.

Bottles

Glass milk bottles can be reused many times over, saving energy. But old smashed bits of glass can be melted down to make new glass, saving energy. Quarrying sand and limestone for new glass is also damaging for the environment. Every tonne of recycled glass saves 1.2 tonnes of sand, soda ash and limestone.

It's only in the last 30 years or so that we've become so hung-up on the 'one-trip' experience. Previously consumers gladly returned drinks bottles to shops (to be refilled and reused) because they were paid to do so. The money-back scheme was abolished in 1971 when the drinks giant Schweppes made the decision to stop using returnable bottles. Thirty years later the threat of global pollution is so serious that it is driving consumers to take their empties by the dozen down to the bottle bank. They don't get paid to do this; it's just that they realise that recycling is better than the 'one-trip'. Schweppes and other drinks manufacturers should take notice!

Recycling bottles is the one bit of recycling many people do. It's encouraging but we can do more.

Aluminium and steel cans

All food and drink cans can be melted down and made into cans again. Recycling aluminium cans uses only about 5 per cent of the energy it takes to make new aluminium from the ground. Four out of every five drink cans in the world are made from pure aluminium. They can easily be recycled but in this country not enough cans are being collected.

In Denmark it is illegal to sell drinks in cans! The Danish government passed this law so that refillable bottles are used as much as possible.

Oil

All car drivers are recommended to change their car oil at least once a year and it is important to dispose of the old oil responsibly. It is actually illegal to pour car oil (also known as sump oil) down the drain. Many drains are directly connected to a river or stream and pollution will occur. It's also illegal to burn used oil in unregulated heaters. Recycling the oil is the safest option. This means processing the oil to remove lead and other contaminants so that the oil can be reused. More councils and high-street garages should provide 'oil banks' for recycling.

Telephone 0800 66 33 66 free to find the location of your nearest used-oil bank. Oil is valuable. Look after it!

Scoop that poop!

The estimated 7.5 million dogs in Britain alone produce 1000 tonnes of excrement each day. As well as being devilishly difficult to wipe off your trainers, dog dirt can seriously damage your health. A worm called toxocara canis, which lives in the gut of dogs, can be passed on to people when dog mess pollutes the soil. Toxocara can infect the eyes and cause blindness. Children under 10 are most at risk.

There's no really environmentally friendly way of disposing of dog dirt. If you're a pet owner encourage your pet to relieve itself in your own back garden. Then bag the mess in small amounts and bin it. Don't leave home without a plastic scoop and a pooper bag! Pooper scooping your pet in public sets a good example that others will follow.

Plastic

Plastic can be recycled, although in 1992 less than 1 per cent of plastic from our household waste actually was. One of the arguments is that there are so many types of plastics that the collection, separation and reprocessing of different plastics is not cost-effective. But this doesn't take into account the price of polluting the planet with the manufacture of billions of new plastic bottles every day. So write to your local authority and ask it to invest in plastic recycling points.

Some supermarkets encourage customers to return their plastic carrier bags to the store where they can be recycled. Waitrose carriers are recycled into plastic garden furniture (there's more about this in the next chapter).

Although Britain has a poor track record on recycling, the future looks a little brighter, thanks to the fact that many designers are now reusing all kinds of materials to make new products. Fashion designer Julie McDonagh, 24, has set up a business making rucksacks and hand-bags from rubber inner tubes. Her bestselling line is a 'spiky bag'. Julie collects the inner tubes from garages around the country. She sews most of the bags herself and for the straps on the larger ones she uses old seat belts.

'In some developing countries they cut up inner tubes to make posts and shoes. I knew most rubber in the UK went to landfill. It would be cheaper, easier and cost-effective for me just to buy sheets of new rubber,' she says. 'But that goes against everything I believe in.' Her bags are waterproof and won't burn or scratch – in fact, they're virtually indestructible.

Left overs

All organic matter, such as fruit and vegetable peelings, stale food, lawn clippings and leaves, and even your pet's waste, can be composted into manure to improve your flower-beds! You can also feed your pets on kitchen scraps.

Don't be a waster! Remember the five R's of recycling:

- Refuse unnecessary packaging
- Return bottles whenever you can; buy returnable bottles if possible
- Reuse as much as you can. Items such as envelopes, bottles and plastic bags can all be reused. Take unwanted clothes to a charity shop
- Repair things rather than throw them away

- Recycle paper, cans and bottles by taking them to your local recycling centre, and compost household waste.

Pollution Busters!

There are lots more ways you can be part of the pollution solution: here's a few ideas to get you going!

- Never drop litter and make a personal pledge to pick up at least three items of litter wherever you see it lying around.
- If you're a real beach bum, make sure you're a tidy one. Take home your rubbish and leave only footprints.
- Pledge to recycle at least a quarter of all your household rubbish.
- Set up your own paper- or can-recycling scheme at school. For information and advice about setting up your own recycling schemes, contact the Community Recycling Network (see Hot Contacts! on page 142).
- Campaign for better recycling facilities in your area. Collect statements from 10 people confirming they would recycle their glass, paper and plastic if recycling stations were within walking distance. Ask 10 friends to each collect 10 statements, too. Then present these statements to your local council and invite the press.
- If your area does have recycling banks but you find they are full, write and ask your council to provide more.
- Some councils collect paper, bottles and cans for recycling from your door. Write and ask your council if they operate this service. If they don't, ask them to start such a scheme.
- Encourage your family to recycle rubbish wherever

possible. Make a big sign reminding them not to throw away anything that could be recycled and slap this on the lid of your kitchen swing bin.

- Compost your kitchen waste. If you haven't got a garden and you're not too squeamish, you can use an indoor worm bin. You need a plastic dustbin and some special compost worms (also called branding or manure worms) – you can buy these from anglers' shops. Feed the worms on food scraps and they will make the scraps into compost for your pot plants.

Use your purse power!

- When you're out shopping look for the 'Recycled' logo. Any products bearing that logo will have been made from recycled material. Look further than paper; you can find a range of items, including clothing, in your high street, all made from recycled products.

- Encourage manufacturers to stop overpackaging their products and so create less waste. If you buy a product that you think is overwrapped, write to the manufacturers and demand simpler wrapping. Tell them you won't be buying that product again until they review their packaging policies.

- Be choosy over your choice of sanpro. Don't buy towels that are individually wrapped. These might seem a good idea because it allows you to carry them individually in your bag. In reality it's unnecessary and wasteful. Brands that are bagged together tend to be cheaper – and just as protective! If you go for these you'll be able to afford a funky make-up purse to take a few towels around with you in your bag. And don't chuck them down the toilet (for all the reasons mentioned in chapter three!). Bag them and bin them instead.

- Find out about reusable sanitary towels and sponges. Contact the Women's Environment Network (see Hot Contacts! on page 148).
- If you have to buy paper products, gen up on the best ones to buy. For example, recycled paper loo rolls are a good idea but in fact a lot of recycled loo roll is made from high-grade waste paper that could be turned into something of higher quality, such as writing paper. Always buy 'post-consumer' recycled paper loo rolls. They're made from old newspapers and magazines.

Fifteen-year-old Kruti Parekh from Maharashtra, western India had enough of foul-smelling rubbish festering on the streets near her home and decided to do something about it. 'The local authorities don't encourage people to recycle their household waste so rag pickers are a common sight in Bombay. They pick through people's rubbish to remove recyclable materials that they can sell on. These pickers split the rubbish bags and spread litter and disease. The garbage attracts swarms of disease-carrying flies, mosquitoes and rats, too. Water supplies can become infected since so many of the buildings' storage tanks are sited at ground level.'

Walking to school Kruti and friends had to cover their noses to avoid the stench from the rotting rubbish. Eventually Kruti decided she had had enough and set up a vermiculture project, composting organic waste using deep-burrowing earthworms. 'Worms process the waste and their excreta contains friendly bacteria that make valuable manure,' she explains. 'Vermiculture increases soil's moisture absorption and helps to prevent land flooding during the heavy monsoons here.'

Having succeeded in encouraging her friends and local temples, schools and canteens to compost their waste, Kruti is now targeting the food-processing, sugar and farming industries, as well as fisheries.

'The environment is a vast area and it can't be one person's job,' says Kruti. 'If many people join their hands then work becomes easy.'

Fifteen-year-old Theresia van der Merwe lives in Benoni, in the Gauteng Province of South Africa, about 35kms east of Johannesburg. Benoni is a fast-developing city with a series of wetlands and lakes running through it that is presently being developed as a lakeside complex with shops, hotels and cinemas.

Theresia belongs to an environmental group called the Wilger Veld Youth Conservation Club. The group was concerned about an area of wetlands called Bullfrog Pan. 'The local council had turned the pan into a dumping ground, polluting it and destroying its wildlife,' she explains. 'Bullfrogs leaving the area are a sure sign of polluted water. And because of the leachate, they had started to leave. Flamingos hadn't visited the site since 1972 and virtually all the birdlife had disappeared. The only remaining bird, the sacred ibis, then took over the dump, picking through the rubbish. Cattle, left to graze the site, had further destroyed the ecosystem.'

Theresia and her fellow pollution-busters ran a campaign to stop the council dumping on the site. Eventually the group's hard work was rewarded when a multi-million rand clean-up programme was actioned to rehabilitate the wetland. 'The rubbish was covered with a metre of good soil and planted with erogrostis grass.

And the erosion canals were covered with bags of soil. We keep monitoring the leachate and regularly testing the water. As soon as we spot any problems we can deal with them immediately.'

Thanks to the group's campaigning, the pan has been designated a protected site. 'We've since renamed the site the "Bullfrog Sanctuary" because it is now home to over 25,000 bullfrogs! It's a major attraction for eco-tourists and has become an "outdoor classroom" for school groups,' Theresia explains.

In June 1998 Anne Mearns, the project founder and organiser, received the Global 500 award from the United Nations Environmental Programme in recognition of her and her group's achievements. The real success here is that what began as a small-scale war on local polluters has had such far-reaching benefits, improving the area not just for the wildlife but for the community as a whole. Theresia is proud to report that, after 27 years in exile, a group of 15 flamingos has now returned to live alongside the bullfrogs.

Chapter 6
Shop 'Til You Drop?

Fact: **20 per cent of the world's population owns over 80 per cent of its wealth and consumes nearly 75 per cent of its material resources.**

Fact: **The us is home to just 6 per cent of the world's population but it consumes 30 per cent of its resources.**

Fact: **20 per cent of the world's population (i.e. the wealthy consumer class) is responsible for over 50 per cent of its air pollution.**

Fact: **One hundred new superstores are built every year. Each one takes up over three hectares of land for the store, the supply roads and other facilities. That's as much as four and a half football pitches!**

> **Buy one, get one free!**
> **Hello boys!**
> **Be afraid, boys, be very afraid!**
> **Nothing comes between me and my new jeans!**
> **Brand new — be ahead of the rest, buy 'em now!**
> **She's gotta have it!**

Consumerism has come to dominate society in the western world. We're constantly encouraged to spend, spend, spend. But contrary to what the adverts would have us believe, buying more new, improved products won't actually make our lives new, improved and better. And while getting to splash your cash can be great fun, we need to think about how to have that fun without harming our planet at the same time.

'We're constantly being bombarded with seductive advertising images telling us that buying more and more will make us sexier, happier and healthier,' explains Anna Thomas, consumerism campaigner at Friends of the Earth. 'The reality is that, far from improving our well-being, consumerism is causing increased pollution, destruction of wildlife habitats and greater tension between the "haves" and the "have nots" of this world.'

Most of us aren't aware of this because the true cost of flying food and clothes in from around the world to our nearest out-of-town superstores is rarely reflected on a product's price tag. For a start there's the polluting air- and road-freight fumes and the energy expended in promoting and distributing and displaying these wares, not to mention the damage we do to the environment shopping by car.

Shopping by car

One of the most worrying things about consumerism is that most people in the West do it by car these days. As recently as the mid-1970s, more people went shopping on foot than by car. But in the past 20 years in the UK alone, car mileage for shopping has trebled – largely thanks to the rise of the out-of-town superstores and shopping malls.

These out-of-town shopping parks may seem convenient and cheap but the environment pays for the savings we make on a trolley full of tasty treats. A recent survey at Asda near High Wycombe found that of 236 customers interviewed, only 4 did not come by car! In fact, about a quarter of car mileage is for shopping or other personal business. It is one of the most polluting uses of the car, because these journeys are too short for catalytic convertors to kick into action. CATs only work when the engine has warmed up, which can take a mile or two.

In little over a decade shopping parks have torn the hearts out of towns and cities that have taken hundreds of years to evolve. Take a stroll down your nearest high street and see how many empty or boarded-up premises you can spot. One third of all households doesn't have access to a car (primarily the poor, the old and the sick), so the closure of local shops reduces their choices enormously.

The next time you climb into the car to drive to a shopping park, try saying this to yourself: 'I'm off to the superstore to close down a few local shops, increase asthma and make life difficult for people without cars.' Because that's what we are actually doing.

It's shopping, Jim, but not as we know it!

It's not all doom and gloom, though. The larger supermarket chains are opening smaller stores on the high street once again, by popular demand. And trendwatchers believe that we may be turning a corner, thanks to new technology.

Internet growth is now so big that most high-street shops are going online so that customers can shop virtually. The idea is that you choose what you want to buy while sitting at home in front of your computer or TV and your goods are then delivered later.

You can already buy a wide range of goods online, from books to cinema tickets, through to getting your weekly supermarket shop delivered to your doorstep, with just a click of a mouse and the beep of your modem! At the moment virtual supermarket shopping is quite restricted. But supermarkets believe it will only be a matter of time before all shopping is done this way – which is certainly something to celebrate. Virtual shopping will have a big impact on pollution: as one delivery van could replace more than a dozen separate supermarket journeys made by families, drastically reducing CO_2 levels.

Supermarkets: not so super after all

In the meantime, while you still have the chance to browse your store, take a look at what's on offer. Even if a fruit or vegetable isn't in season where you live, you'll be able to buy it. Supermarkets import fruit and vegetables from hotter climates in countries thousands of miles away so they are in stock all year round. For example, in the UK we can grow strawberries, plums and lettuces in summer only. But browse round the fruit and vegetable counters of a big supermarket in winter and you'll find strawberries from South America, juice from Honduran oranges and green beans from the Gambia. These tasty products are part of an unsustainable food system.

Many of the workers growing foods on plantations are short of food themselves, because they are paid a pittance. Child labour is often used to keep prices low. On the pollution side, it takes up to four litres of fuel to carry just one kilo of fruit and veg from California to Europe. Of course, it's great sometimes to be able to buy blackberries or papaya, but before you put them in your basket, think about the wider implications of the 'global supermarket'. The people who benefit most from it are transport and oil companies, food manufacturers and supermarkets – not you, the consumer.

What you decide to buy when you shop could change the world. Big supermarkets only put things on their shelves that they can sell – and sell fast! So by using your purse power and refusing to buy eco-unfriendly products you can force supermarkets to replace them with ones that are better for the planet.

Say No to Unwanted Bags (SNUB)

You can improve your green power by reusing carrier bags – or refusing them in the first place. Plastic carriers, which are often only used once, are an environmental problem. Put it this way: they may come free but they are costing us the earth because they:

- are made from oil (a non-renewable fossil fuel)
- take hundreds of years to degrade
- are rarely reused and often end up as litter, where they can endanger wildlife.

So, if someone offers you a plastic carrier bag, just SNUB 'em!

Some supermarkets are encouraging shoppers to reuse plastic carriers – and not before time. Each year British food retailers give away enough carrier bags to cover the whole of London with more than 600 layers of bags. In 1996 Waitrose gave away 150 million carrier bags, enough to stretch around the world two and a half times. Production of those bags uses the same amount of oil as 57,000 cars driving from London to Glasgow. So in 1997 Waitrose launched a campaign to encourage shoppers to reuse their carrier bags by introducing the 'Bag for Life' scheme. Customers pay 10p for a larger, extra-strong carrier that should last for up to 10 shopping trips or so. When the bag breaks it is replaced for free and recycled into plastic furniture such as vandal-proof park benches. To complete this cycle, Waitrose is installing these into its supermarkets – so customers get the benefit!

Within the first six months of launching this scheme Waitrose noticed a reduction of between 12 and 28 per cent in normal carrier bag use. This means that between 40 and 65 million fewer carrier bags are given away in a year. Sainsbury's has run a 'penny-back' scheme, encouraging shoppers to reuse their carriers, for several years. For each bag reused the customer gets a penny, which they are encouraged to donate to charity. Sainsbury's estimates that its customers reuse about 7.5 per cent of carrier bags; that's equivalent to saving one and a half million bags every week, or 30,000 gallons of oil and 30 tonnes of plastic! Think how much more could be saved if every shop did this. The Body Shop is committed to ensuring 60 per cent of its UK customers don't take a plastic bag. Help them by always SNUB-ing when you're shopping.

Animal matters

Whether you're a meat eater or not, you must have noticed that most superstores have entire aisles dedicated to meat and meat products. That's because people now expect meat as a daily part of their diet, although this never used to be the case. When your grandparents were young, meat was a Sunday treat. Today, however, school canteens and fast-food restaurants are brimming with beef burgers, chicken nuggets and turkey dinosaurs – at the planet's expense.

To satisfy our increased appetite for meat and animal products, many farms at home and abroad are rearing animals intensively in cruel conditions. For example, cows, which naturally graze on grass, are now being kept in sheds, fed large doses of antibiotics and chemicals to make them grow and are often forced to eat special food that contains meat.

Six hundred million broiler chickens are 'grown' each year in the UK in light-filled sheds to trick them into growing twice as fast as they normally would. Six hundred million chicks make an awful lot of polluting waste but not once in the seven short weeks from hatching until their slaughter date are their sheds cleaned out.

But it's not only animals that are being farmed intensively. Today, our crops are farmed this way, too. Tonnes of bug-zapping pesticides are sprayed onto crops, and soils are soaked with fertiliser to bump up the crop. This kills off butterflies, birds and flowers, and pollutes the environment, as we've already seen.

As pesticides get absorbed by plants and then by the animals that feed on them, in addition to the antibiotics and other chemicals, pollutants become dangerously concentrated at the top of the food-chain, i.e. in us humans. Recent research has shown that sometimes pesticide residues as high as six times the recommended safety level can be found in intensively farmed food. By law most farmers have to spray or paint strong chemicals on to farm animals' coats to keep bugs at bay. But these are so strong they can make the farmers quite ill. Sheep-dip containing organophosphates causes the same kind of health problems associated with Gulf War Syndrome, which affects many of the soldiers who were exposed to high levels of insecticides during the 1991 Gulf War against Iraq.

Frankenstein food

Pesticides and herbicides are not the only form of pollution affecting our food supplies. Genetic engineering is a recent development in food technology that allows scientists to take genes from one organism and put them into another. This changes the way the organism develops, making new types of plants and animals. It allows genes to be crossed between organisms that could never breed naturally. A gene from a fish, for example, has been put into a tomato. No, that's not a joke; apparently it makes them resistant to frost! Scientists identified the gene in the fish that stopped it freezing in icy water and transferred it to a tomato, to give the tomato the same property. These 'frankenstein foods' don't taste better than ordinary foods and aren't any cheaper. In short, there's no reason why we, as consumers, would want them. But they have been created by scientists to resist pesticides and disease and to stay fresh longer on our supermarket shelves.

Genetically engineered soya and maize have been quietly included in at least 60 per cent of the foods we've been eating, such as bread, pasta, pizza and ready meals.

They're rarely labelled as such; if they're present in small enough quantities, they legally don't have to be. Potentially, genetically modified, or GM, soya and maize products could also be entering meat and dairy produce via GM animal feed (which also doesn't have to be labelled).

Like other forms of pollution, genetic engineering is about putting profits before the planet. Releasing genetically engineered organisms into the environment is indeed a form of pollution because it will disrupt the natural biodiversity of our plant life. Genetically modified crop plants can transfer to wild plants to create 'super-weeds'. Between 1997 and 1999, GM crops, from potatoes and strawberries to oilseed rape, were grown in over 500 test sites across Britain.

No one knows exactly what impact these crops will have on the environment and the risks to our health are still uncertain. Many of these foods may be safe, but it could take many years before we can know this for sure. It is certainly already causing problems: recently a soybean was mixed genetically with a brazil nut and, guess what? It caused allergies in people allergic to nuts. Fortunately this was discovered before the product was put out onto the market but will we always be so lucky? Friends of the Earth is equally concerned about the fact that genetically engineered maize has been created with an antibiotic-resistant gene. What if humans and animals who eat this maize develop a resistance to antibiotics, too?

Fortunately, thanks to pressure from campaign groups including Friends of the Earth, Greenpeace and others, most of the major supermarket chains are going GM-free on their own brands. And UK manufacturers are phasing out GM ingredients from their foods, because we, the consumers, have shown that we won't buy them. But Britain is planning to start growing GM crops even though we don't yet know how dangerous they might be. So there's still some way to go.

Can the can

While we're on the subject of alerting you to the potential dangers lurking in your local supermarket, take a fresh look at tinned food. As you probably know, tinned food loses vitamins and minerals in the canning process. What less people are aware of is that buying and eating canned food can expose you to polluting chemicals. Many (but not all) tin cans are lined with BPA, or bisphenol. This chemical is a gender bender (see chapter four) and very low doses have been shown to cause prostate problems in mice. Worryingly, BPA has been found to leach from the tin lining into the food within the can. Since there's no way of knowing which cans are lined with BPA it's best to avoid tinned foods until this chemical is banned from food packaging.

'Real Food' for a real future

As you'll have noticed as you read through this chapter the many and varied problems affecting our food are actually all part of one bigger issue: namely, that our food production system puts profit before the needs of the planet and its people. Friends of the Earth is calling for a return to safe, healthy, tasty food that provides a good deal for you and for the people who produce it, and for the planet, too. In short, a return to 'Real Food'.

Real Food is affordable food that's free from:

- pesticides
- antibiotics
- artificial growth hormones
- food-poisoning bacteria such as salmonella and some strains of E. coli
- GM crops and ingredients
- chemical additives and flavourings and other contamination.

As mentioned earlier, we still don't know exactly how harmful GMs and other contaminates such as pesticides may be. Their real effects won't be known for two or three generations. What we do know already, though, is that eating more organically grown fresh fruit and vegetables and less processed foods (which contain sugar, salt, fat and animal products) significantly reduces your chances of getting heart disease. And that can't be bad. Organic food comes pretty close to Real Food. Grown locally, seasonal organic food matches the description to a T. It's guaranteed free from pesticides, antibiotics, pathogens, hormones – and genetically engineered or modified ingredients.

Organic produce is better for wildlife and the countryside. Growing food without artificial chemicals helps stop pollution of the soil, rivers and crops and so helps protect wildlife. And it puts you in the driving seat. Buying locally puts you in touch with producers and brings you much closer to your food. Using a vegetable box scheme run from a nearby farm is one of the cheapest ways of going organic – and you don't have to leave home! Supermarket organic food is expensive because it is sold pre-packed not loose (it has to be, otherwise it would be impossible to distinguish it from non-organic food at the checkout). Started by the Exeter Friends of the Earth group in 1991, there are now over 400 box schemes delivering to an estimated 50,000 families each week. They normally offer different sized boxes, and their produce is locally produced, fresh and usually organic.

An organic future

Organic farming is pioneering the way for a healthier, pollution-free future. Between the years 1992 and 1997 the organic market trebled. Buying locally grown food supports organic farmers and this way of farming means fewer pollution problems for us all. Eating fresh, locally grown organic food is better for your health. The downside of organic food is that it tends to be more expensive than intensively grown food. This wouldn't be the case if governments and more consumers supported organic farming. For more info about organic and sustainably produced food contact Sustain: the alliance for better food and farming (see Hot Contacts! on page 146).

Five steps to eco-friendlier shopping:
1. Buy locally produced goods from local shops and markets.
2. Walk to the shops, or go by bike or public transport rather than by car. If you have no choice but to go by car, car share. A car full of people who all want to

go to the same destination is less polluting than four empty ones!
3. If you have a choice, buy things in materials you can recycle locally. Don't buy overpackaged products.
4. Buy things that can be reused – time and time again.
5. Before you buy something, stop and think if it will last a long time. If it breaks or starts wearing out, can it be easily repaired? (It's better to mend things instead of throwing them out!)

By shopping more carefully you can really do your bit to help the planet. For example, always buy milk in glass bottles rather than in paper cartons, which are usually thrown away after being used once. And choose low-grade loo paper made from old newspapers and magazines that have little use once they've been finished with. Use (or encourage your family to follow) our good buys shopping list below and your weekly shop needn't cost the earth.

Good buys:
- organic meat and fish
- organic milk, eggs and cheese
- products that haven't been tested on animals
- recycled paper
- products that come in reusable or recyclable packaging
- fair-trade foods
- organically grown produce
- energy-efficient light-bulbs
- pump-action sprays (instead of aerosols)
- the most energy-efficient washing machines, ghetto blasters, etc
- rechargeable batteries.

When shopping, keep an eye out for 'green cons'. Manufacturers know that shoppers feel good buying green products and often promote their products as being environmentally friendly by stretching the truth. For example, washing-powder manufacturers often draw consumers' attention to the environmental information on their packets. Labelling detergent with the words 'biodegradable – breaks down in the environment' is a con to make themselves look eco-friendly; by law all detergents have to be at least 80 per cent biodegradable within 19 days.

Paper products often carry misleading messages about 'sustainable forestry'. This often means 'factory forests': dense plantations of little value for wildlife or local inhabitants. And keep an eye out for products labelled with the phrase: 'This packaging can be recycled' – unless people make the effort to take it to a recycling point, it won't be! Sometimes, even if you want to recycle something, there may not be facilities near you to do so. For example, there still are practically no plastic-recycling schemes. You're better off buying a similar product that comes in recycled or refillable packaging.

The EU has a green-labelling scheme that takes into account the environmental impact of a product throughout its life cycle. This includes the extraction of raw materials, energy used to make it, its energy efficiency when in use and its disposal (is it reuseable or recycled, or is it simply thrown away?). At the time of writing this scheme is voluntary. Friends of the Earth believes it should be compulsory!

Don't forget, the more you and your family shop wisely and use your purse power, the easier it will become for everyone! And you'll be doing your bit for the pollution solution, too.

The real solution: cutting back on consumerism

However much all of us enjoy shopping and however hard we try to become better shoppers we've got to take a reality check on the whole consumerism craze. Ultimately we all need to stop and think about our material consumption and cut it back where we can if we're going to reduce pollution.

Being a green consumer is a good way to start. Green consumerism is linked closely with ethical consumerism, although this considers a wider variety of issues, such as whether or not the manufacturer invests in the arms trade or has supported oppressive regimes. Ethical consumerism supports 'fair trade', which means paying the people who produce food and products a decent wage and not destroying their environment. Ethical consumerism is becoming more important as the world's governments release their power to multinational corporations. You can find out more about ethical consumerism from the pressure group Enough. Enough runs an anti-consumerism campaign in the UK each year, including a 'No Shop Day' when consumers are encouraged to spend a day buying nothing (harder than it sounds!).

Mahatma Gandhi, the Indian leader famous for helping the subcontinent break free from British rule and imperialism in the 1940s, famously said, 'There is enough on earth for everybody's need, but not for everyone's greed.'

A consumer society is all about wanting new things.

It's something we pick up from a very early age. Almost before they can put pen to paper children write a mental Christmas- or birthday-present list. How many people do you know that could honestly claim that they have everything they need? Unfortunately manufacturers and the advertising industry constantly feed our desire for 'stuff'. On some level most of us understand that human happiness shouldn't be about what kind of trainers you own or how much money you earn and spend. Contentment is more about being happy with who you are and how you treat people.

It's time we all thought carefully about our wants and needs and tried to curb our consuming, for our happiness and possibly our very survival.

Pollution Busters!

What you can do personally

- Become a sensible shopper. Go green, curb pollution and you can cruise the high street without guilt!
- Help your community: support your local shops. These might charge a little more for some products but save you time and the costs of travelling to out-of-town shopping parks.
- Avoid GM foods. It's not as easy as it sounds but will become easier since almost all the leading supermarkets are going GM-free on their own brands. Each chain is working to a different timescale, however, so ask your local branch manager to advise you. Food manufacturers will be introducing a GM-free label for use on their processed foods but again this may take some time. Until then, buy fresh fruit and vegetables.

Organic or not, these are GM-free.

- Eat more locally grown vegetables instead of meat. (Beware of soya products; they're imported from the other side of the world and so guzzle up lots of food miles! And they may be genetically modified, too.)

- Find out if there's a box scheme of locally grown organic fruit and vegetables in your area. The Soil Association (see Hot Contacts! on page 146) will be able to tell you where you can buy locally produced organic fruit, vegetables and meat. Look for the Soil Association symbol. It is awarded to producers who do not use dangerous chemicals or intensive farming.

- Buy direct from the farmer, at a local farmers' market if there's one near you. Hugely successful in the US, traditional in countries like France and Spain, farmers' markets are now catching on in the UK.

- Don't buy meat that has been intensively farmed. Choose free-range or organic meat instead. If you don't want to eat meat you can be a vegetarian and still be perfectly healthy. Find out more in *The Livewire Guide to Going, Being and Staying Veggie!* by Juliet Gellatley, or by contacting VIVA! (Vegetarian International Voice for Animals; see Hot Contacts! on page 147).

- Write to your local supermarket branch manager and ask her/him to stock more locally produced organic foods.

- Or grow your own! Bypass the food industry altogether and grow food in your own garden, or allotment. It's a fun way of guaranteeing yourself fresh organic food, without clocking up any 'food miles'.

- Restyle yourself with jumble-sale chic. Once in a

while it's worth shopping in charity shops; you'll be amazed at the good things that turn up there.

- Always buy energy-efficient appliances. If you must use batteries, make sure they are rechargeable.

- Write to local businesses asking what they are doing to conserve energy. Keep an eye out for shops that leave their doors open all day. Think of all the energy that's pouring out onto the street. Write and remind them how polluting this is and ask them to become more energy efficient.

- Keep an eye out for green cons and don't let the companies making misleading claims get away with it! In the UK you can report all green cons that appear in printed advertisements (i.e. in newspapers, magazines or on advertising hoardings) to the Advertising Standards Authority. The Independent Television Commission handles complaints about advertisements broadcast on television. (See Hot Contacts! on page 144–145 for further details).

- Encourage your favourite shops to rethink their plastic-bag policy. Ask them not to hand out bags to customers automatically. Forward-thinking shops such as the Body Shop ask their customers whether they want a bag – most people don't.

- Reduce, Reuse, Refill, Recycle: choose products that can be reused, refilled or recycled, for maximum purse power! You can reduce waste by always buying products with as little packaging as possible (see chapter five for more details).

- Buy direct. There are hundreds of thouands of mail-order firms worldwide who will deliver products straight to your door.

If you have access to the internet, shop 'virtually' wherever possible. Contact your local superstore for more details. If it's not yet operating an internet home-delivery service write to the manager requesting that it does so. The more demand stores have for this service the quicker it should materialise.

And last but by no means least, think before you buy. Think about what you need, not what you want. You could find yourself saving pounds – and being a whole lot happier into the bargain!

Encouraging the government to act

Write to your MP and state your concerns about genetically engineered foods. Ask for a moratorium (temporary ban) until government research is complete. And ask what the government is doing to support organic agriculture.

Press for Real Food in your workplace and/or schools. We want food served in all restaurants, cafés, schools, colleges and workplaces to be guaranteed GM-free. After all, the government has banned GMs in its own Houses of Parliament cafés and restaurants. If they're not good enough for our politicians they're not good enough for us! Group together with your friends and/or work colleagues to get GM food banned in your local café, college and workplace. It works. The Leicester FOE group recently persuaded the city's council to ban GM-foods from all school meals, after a campaign that proved nine out of ten pupils didn't want them.

Fifteen-year-old Gemma Smith from Montpelier in Bristol has been a member of Friends of the Earth for a year.

Together with her friends she set up Cake (Constructive Action in a Knackered Environment), running local campaigns, delivering leaflets, organising petitions and protesting against polluting projects. Gemma is concerned about genetically modified food polluting our food-chains and has made a video to alert schools and colleges to the dangers of GM food.

'I absolutely don't agree with GM food. But if food companies continue developing and using it they must keep the public informed about where those foods are on sale. Everyone should be able to make an informed choice about the food they're buying; they need to know what has gone into it and the costs to the environment.

'I try to buy foods from health shops and from farm shops when I can afford it. I'm lucky to have an organic bakery and health-food shop within 10 minutes walk of my house. I believe the government should subsidise organic food. Right now it is expensive and you have to go out of your way to buy it. I'd like to see organic produce readily available at a wider range of places.

'Transport and food are inextricably linked as pollution issues. Buying locally grown products from local shops and farms helps cut pollution. When local farmers are producing fruit and vegetables in season it is madness to drive to an out-of-town supermarket to buy something that has been flown in from the other side of the world!'

Chapter 7

Power is Polluting...

Fact: **World energy use has doubled in the last 25 years.**

Fact: **The average person in the UK uses more than 10 times more energy than the average person in India.**

Fact: **Every year, the world consumes as much oil as it takes nature one million years to create.**

Fact: **Every year, accidental and deliberate pollution dumps two and a half million tonnes of oil in our oceans.**

We need energy for almost everything we do, from cooking our food to heating our homes and powering industry. Unfortunately, all the energy that we're constantly generating, using and wasting (and we'll come to that a bit later!) comes at a price: second only to cars, power is the biggest source of pollution on this planet.

Industrialised countries use about 70 per cent of the world's energy and fossil fuels. Every year each man, woman and child in the UK uses an amount of energy equal to more than 18,411 litres of oil – that's about 51 bath-tubs full! All this energy ends up disappearing into thin air. The average UK household is responsible for the emission of seven and a half tonnes of carbon dioxide into the atmosphere each year.

So where do we get our energy from? And what happens to the environment when we use it? At present in the UK 91 per cent of our energy comes from fossil fuels such as coal, oil and gas. Fossil fuels are so called because they were formed over millions of years from the fossilised remains of dead animals and plants. These are burnt in power stations to give us electricity for homes and industries. Unfortunately, burning fossil fuels releases carbon dioxide into the atmosphere, contributing to some of the world's greatest pollution problems, such as global warming (there's more about this later) and acid rain. We have to seek alternatives to fossil fuels because we can't afford to burn them any more!

Nuclear energy

Nuclear power is sometimes cited as a cleaner form of energy. It doesn't directly produce carbon dioxide or acid–rain gases but it does produce highly dangerous radioactive waste that can cause cancer, birth deformities and even kill. Radioactive waste gives off radiation that is so deadly it must be kept out of harm's way for hundreds of thousands of years. Yet there's no way of doing this safely and not much evidence that all the world's nuclear powers are rigorous in the careful disposal of their waste.

For example, the Chinese government recently confessed to dumping nuclear waste in Tibet, a country they have occupied since 1949. A 20km² dump of radioactive pollutants is sited near the shores of Lake Kokonor. It's believed that this may have contaminated underground water supplies, as local doctors have reported a high incidence of children with cancer.

In the UK there's a higher than normal incidence of leukaemia in children in the area around Sellafield, a big nuclear-fuel plant in Cumbria, England. In southern Iraq there are reports of a huge rise in the amount of birth deformities since the 1991 Gulf War. These birth deformities, which include babies being born without limbs, eyes and even without heads, are thought to be due to the increased amount of radioactive uranium released from missiles fired in the Kuwait conflict.

The threat of an accident at a nuclear plant (or the detonation of a nuclear weapon) is almost too frightening to think about. The Chernobyl disaster that occurred on 26 April 1986 in the Ukraine is often cited as one of the world's worst human-made disasters. Even though the number of deaths directly associated with Chernobyl is relatively low – 31 people died, 28 of whom died from radiation – it is estimated that during the next 30 years or so delayed deaths caused by radiation-induced cancers will eventually total 1600. Immediately after the accident a huge cloud of radioactive material drifted over Europe and the effects were felt thousands of miles away. In North Wales, for example, radioactive debris rained on sheep. Two months later the UK government slapped a ban on herds of 'radioactive' sheep. Thousands of British farmers were prevented from selling their herds for slaughter. The number of affected sheep has reduced over the years but by 1999 (13 years later) thousands of sheep were still showing high levels of radioactivity.

Thousands of people in the Ukraine are still suffering the after-effects of that disaster. Babies are being born with terrible deformities, and the incidence of thyroid cancer has greatly increased. Even more worryingly, the concrete casing laid over the reactor to seal it is said to be on the point of collapse, threatening yet another nuclear disaster. Even though this is too horrible to think about, with over 350 nuclear reactors operating in the world, the chances are that there will be another major accident within our lifetime.

Only 3 per cent of UK electricity is produced by using nuclear power, although other nations, such as France, use more. Fifty years ago governments claimed that nuclear-power would be the cheapest form of energy but it hasn't quite worked out that way. The safety costs of maintaining nuclear-power stations and safely disposing of nuclear waste are very high. Nuclear power has always been more expensive than electricity generated from coal. Nearly 10p in every pound on your electricity bill is used to subsidise the price of running a nuclear-power programme. France, which has the world's most ambitious nuclear programme, has one of the biggest nuclear debts, too; at the last count this stood at more than £23 billion.

What's the alternative?

We need a radical change in the way we generate and use energy – an energy revolution – if we are to meet our energy needs and protect the planet now and for future generations. Friends of the Earth believes that the energy revolution can come through investment in sustainable, 'renewable' power sources as alternatives to fossil fuels, which are cleaner, safer and – more importantly – won't run out! Renewable energy captures the inexhaustible energy of the wind, water, wave and sun. It already provides about one fifth of the world's electricity and must be developed for the future. Solar power is already widely used in a number of countries, such as Japan (with over one and a half million homes in Tokyo), and Australia. In Israel two thirds of all homes have solar water heaters. The UK, which is roughly only half as sunny as some of the sunniest parts of the world, still receives enough sun power to heat millions of homes and their water.

Britain's wind and wave power was used hundreds of years ago. Water-mills and windmills were a common sight and as far back as the Middle Ages, tidal water-mills were used by the sea, driven by ponds that filled at high tides. There was a mill on London Bridge in the 17th century that got half of its power from the tidal movements of the river between the arches of the bridge.

Sadly, these days very little of the UK's energy is generated by wind or wave power, despite the fact that our resources are among the best in the world. For example, a tidal-power generator sited at the Bristol Channel could produce about 5.5 per cent of Britain's present electricity needs. And it is estimated that wind energy alone could supply at least 20 per cent of the UK's electricity, using off-shore wind turbines as well as those sited on land. Every unit of electricity produced by a wind turbine avoids at least half a kilogram of CO_2 being emitted into the atmosphere. In Denmark, wind energy already produces more than 7 per cent of its electricity needs, avoiding the need to build further conventional, polluting power stations. However, over 70 per cent of wind-power proposals in the UK have been turned down for planning permission since 1995.

Who in their right mind would put up resistance to developing fuels that would help save the planet? Most of the objections to wind power have come from NIMBYs: local people who object to proposed windmill sites on the basis that it will spoil their view. The NIMBY (Not In My Back Yard) attitude is somewhat shortsighted. As Nick Goddall, chief executive of the British Wind Energy Association, says, 'Perhaps we should recognise that "visual impact" is a matter of judgement, without "right" and "wrong" answers. In the trade-off between environmental benefits and visual amenity, which is more important? Wind energy is cheap, environmentally friendly and should make a significant contribution to our needs.

'Wind energy, together with other renewables and energy efficiency, are all essential in moving towards sustainability. Even British Energy, one of the UK's largest nuclear generators, has stated that "if there is to be a sustainable future, the world must move to using more renewable energy." In the UK we have the greatest wind resource of any European country. We know how to make large quantities of electricity from the wind. We should use that resource. For our children's sakes.'

There is very real resistance to curbing our use of fossil fuels from companies who are in the business of extracting, processing and selling them. Massive international companies are putting up serious opposition to adopting carbon-dioxide cuts and a renewable energy programme, because billions of dollars are at stake. These companies are not faceless corporations; they're high-street names: Esso, Ford, Vauxhall (General Motors) and Texaco. They belong to a lobby group called the Global Climate Coalition (GCC), which is arguing that climate change action will damage the economy. This is despite evidence that global climate change is one of the most serious threats facing our planet, and that action to halt it can actually create jobs and bring economic benefits.

The GCC has run advertising campaigns questioning the science behind climate-change predictions. It has also successfully persuaded the US senate not to agree to the 6 per cent cut in greenhouse-gas emissions set out in the Kyoto Treaty at the 1997 Climate-Change Summit.

So much damage to the environment is caused by our use of energy that it makes no sense to use more energy than we need. Yet that's exactly what we're doing. World energy use has doubled in the last 25 years but much of it is wasted. For example, nearly every power station in Britain wastes more than half of the energy in coal, oil and uranium when it converts it into electricity. The waste comes out as steam, allowed to escape into the atmosphere via huge cooling towers. By changing the design of power stations, this energy could be put to work instead. For example, Combined Heat and Power (or CHP) stations trap waste heat that can be piped directly to heat local homes and factories. CHP schemes are common in European cities but have been under-used in the UK.

The good news among all the bad is that things are improving on the renewable energy front. More than 200,000 wind turbines have been built worldwide over the last 10 years to generate electricity. And new forms of renewable energy are being developed. Scientists are experimenting with a source called geothermal energy.

This utilises the heat in the top 10km of the earth's crust by pumping water through cracks in deep layers of rock! They are also looking at biomass, or burning organic matter to generate energy. For example, agricultural waste and energy crops such as willow and poplar can be burnt without polluting the environment. Even though this burning releases carbon dioxide it will be absorbed again when the crops are growing.

Europe's first commercial wood-fuelled power plant near Selby in North Yorkshire will generate electricity using wood chips from forest residues and specially grown willow coppice. It will produce enough electricity to meet the daily demands of more than 18,000 people and reduce emissions of greenhouse gases.

Wind energy is the cheapest form of renewable energy, though this is partly because there has been more research and development into it than other forms and because investors have more confidence in it. In theory it is possible to harness energy from waves, although no fully functioning wave-power stations exist anywhere in the world to date. Setting it up from scratch is a highly expensive enterprise. Some companies in Norway, Indonesia and Japan, for example, are, however, doing just this. In the UK a company called ART is building a prototype off Inverness in Scotland to explore wave power, but government-funded wave power in the UK is still many years off.

Helping the earth begins at home

Support the energy revolution by putting pressure on your parents or flatmates to choose an electricity supplier that generates power from renewable sources. Green energy may be more expensive than fossil-fuel energy but it is the best deal for us all in the long term. Other energy doesn't reflect the true cost of pollution or the price the planet pays for its ghastly side-effects. Friends of the Earth hopes that consumer demand for green energy will force electricity companies to invest in and supply more renewable energy and price it competitively. Contact Friends of the Earth for a list of green companies, as described in the free *Guide to Buying Green Energy*.

Pollution Busters!

What you can do personally

Massive investment in renewable energy will help curb pollution. However, there are masses of ways we can all help save energy and support the energy revolution.

Be a super saver!

Make a personal commitment to saving as much energy as possible – and stop wasting it! There are plenty of ways to save energy without going to bed an hour earlier and getting up an hour later. Here are some easy ways you can help take the heat off the planet:

- turn it off! Only real energy wasters leave the TV on standby. A set on standby can still use a quarter of the energy it uses when it's on. It's estimated that if all the appliances in the UK were left on standby just for one hour it would take two large power stations to power them. So don't be a couch potato; get up and switch it off properly.

- become a sneaky switcher. Turn off lights in empty rooms and all electrical appliances if they're not in use.
- if you feel chilly put on a cardigan instead of turning up the central heating!
- don't even think about opening a window while your central heating is on – instead get the heating turned down.
- don't use more hot water than you need – take showers instead of baths.
- only fill the kettle with as much water as you need.
- connect your CD player or stereo to the mains whenever possible. Running appliances on batteries is highly polluting. If you must use batteries, make sure they are rechargeable.
- invest in a wind-up radio – the eco-friendly way to get up to speed with the charts or catch up with world affairs.

Saving energy saves money

Persuade your parents or flatmates to cut your household's energy consumption. Taking energy-saving steps in your home now means cheaper fuel bills for years to come. It's worth reminding people about this since some energy-saving measures will actually cost money. But you will get that money eventually deducted off your fuel bills. For example, if you buy a puffa jacket for your water-heating cylinder you'll get your money back within a year, and from then on you'll save money on your bills. Some steps won't cost you a penny but will still save you pounds. For example, turning the thermostat down by one degree, or using an hour less heating a day, saves about £32 a year.

Space- and water-heating together account for 75 per cent of your home's fuel bills. So the cost element is probably the best way to persuade your parents or flat-mates to tackle your home's heating system and expend less polluting power. Here are some easy ways how:

- insulate or improve the insulation in the loft
- turn down the thermostat by a few degrees
- draught-proof the doors and windows
- lag the hot-water tank
- turn off radiators in empty rooms
- fit aluminium foil behind radiators to reflect heat back into the room and so bump up their heating power
- buy energy-efficient, compact fluorescent light-bulbs.
- when necessary replace any appliances (fridges, freezers, cookers, TVs, etc.) with energy-efficient ones.

Work out how and when your family uses the most energy at home. Check your electricity and gas meters every three hours for one day. You'll notice that the meters move faster when you're using more energy. Work out what activities (cooking, washing, etc.) guzzle up the most gas or electricity. Then ask your gas or electricity board for advice on doing these activities more energy-efficiently.

To find out how many kilograms of climate-changing carbon dioxide your household is producing, just multiply the number of kilowatt hours shown on your fuel bills by 0.19 for gas and 0.83 for electricity. Now aim to cut this by a third – just for a week. Once you've seen how easy it is to save energy and money you won't want to stop. Tot up the cost of the savings you're making and ask your parents to give you this amount as a clothing allowance.

Another way to beat pollution in your own home is to have a renewable-energy system installed. Forty-five thousand households in the UK now have solar-heating systems (this form of heating is especially good for heating swimming pools). In hot, sunny countries solar power can supply all a household's hot water and electricity needs. In the UK where there is less sunlight all year round, solar-heating systems can meet around half their users' annual household hot-water needs. Even people who can't afford the expense of installing a new water-heating system in their home can make use of solar-powered garden lights, or pumps and fountains, for example. Solar-powered garden lights charge up during the day to provide up to seven hours continuous light. You can buy them for around £70 and you'll be guaranteed to have no running costs and no pollution guilt!

Encouraging the government to act

New regulations and greater investment are needed to boost green energy and energy efficiency, particularly as the government is committed to reducing carbon-dioxide emissions by 20 per cent by the year 2010. Friends of the Earth thinks electricity companies should be legally obliged to source some of their electricity from renewable-energy schemes.

What you can do personally

- Write to your MP and demand more government support for renewables and energy efficiency, to cut greenhouse gases and tackle the threat of climate change.

- Write to your MP saying that you want the government to invest more money in renewable energy and to force the electricity companies to get a percentage of their electricity from renewable sources every year.
- Write to your local council and ask it to check its purchasing records to ensure that it is not using significant quantities of ordinary light-bulbs that could be replaced with low-energy compact fluorescent lamps. Some use 80 per cent less energy than ordinary ones and last far longer.
- Last, but by no means least, put pressure on those companies in the Global Climate Coalition. Write and let them know that you are worried that they are opposing steps to halt climate change. For more information on member companies write to Friends of the Earth at the address at the front of this book.
- Support your local renewable-energy scheme; a wind farm, for example. Write a letter to the local paper explaining why it is so good and why it should be supported.

Chapter 8

... And Causing Climate Change

Fact: **The golden and harlequin toads have become extinct in rainforests in Costa Rica because of decreased rainfall.**

Fact: **Scientists have noticed sharp declines in the numbers of the adelie penguin in Antarctica because warmer weather has led to fewer very cold winters, when heavy sea- (or pack-) ice occurs.**

Fact: **Rapid temperature increases in the Arctic are expected to push climate and vegetation zones northward at an astounding rate of up to 341 miles over 100 years.**

Fact: **In 1998, the hottest year on record, environmental refugees outnumbered those displaced by war for the first time. Fifty-eight per cent of the world's refugees were fleeing natural disasters.**

Warning: if you've found some of the facts in this book a little daunting, brace yourself: there's worse still to come. Pollution is, as you've already read, responsible for a whole bag of problems, from giving us sore throats and asthma, and eating away some of the world's historic monuments, to turning male fish and other creatures female. It's also creating planetary problems on an immensely worrying scale. Some of the world's leading scientists are now convinced that pollution is responsible for climate change or global warming, and it's destroying the planet's all-important ozone layer.

Global warming and ozone depletion are two separate and distinct problems in their own right. They are linked because they're both caused by human-made pollutants and, if left unchecked, they could potentially create disastrous problems for the planet, unless we take action to stop the rot!

The greenhouse effect and global climate change

Over the last 100 years average global temperatures have increased by around half a degree. In the 1970s scientists began to grapple with the idea that human-made pollution was seriously changing the earth's climate. A decade later they began to worry that the earth would overheat and called this phenomenon 'global warming'. Their message began to get through to the rest of the world in the late 1980s after unusual weather patterns prevailed.

Scientists believe the planet is getting warmer because the industrialised world, with its millions of factories and millions of cars, is pumping more 'greenhouse gases' (carbon dioxide, methane, nitrous oxide and CFCs) into the atmosphere than ever before. Greenhouse gases are so-called because they make an insulating layer around the earth, like the glass in a greenhouse, to trap in the heat of the sun's rays. This is called the 'greenhouse effect', a term coined way back in 1827 by a French mathematician and scientist, Jean-Baptiste Fournier, who noticed that certain gases trapped heat in the atmosphere.

The greenhouse effect isn't in itself worrying: without it the earth would be an incredible 32°C chillier than it is now and life as we know it could not exist. But before this century there were just about the right amount of greenhouse gases in the atmosphere to keep the earth at the right temperature. Levels are higher today, however, than at any other time in history. In fact they're so high now that it's almost as though another layer of double glazing has been added around the earth. The very coldest parts of the planet, the polar ice caps, have started to melt!

More than 2000 of the world's leading climate scientists who report to the Inter-Governmental Panel on Climate Change (IPCC) have predicted that, if we fail to take action, global temperatures may increase by up to 3.5°C by the year 2100. This would mean that sea levels could increase between 13cm and 95cm between now and 2100.

How global warming will cause havoc with the world

Global sea level is already rising. Over the last hundred years it has risen by between 10cm and 25cm. As the earth keeps on getting hotter, the ice caps will keep melting and as a result low-lying parts of the world, such as the Maldives and Bangladesh, may be drowned. The most vulnerable parts of the UK include the coastal lowlands of East Anglia, the Thames estuary, Teeside, parts of Wales and coastal Lancashire. Virtually all the UK's coastal nuclear-power stations are potentially at risk from sea level over the next century.

But global warming isn't just about the earth getting warmer. As the earth's climate changes, more extreme weather events, such as droughts, torrential rain, floods, hurricanes and heatwaves, are predicted to happen. Of course, there have always been freak-weather conditions but over the last 30 years the number of floods, droughts, storms and heatwaves has trebled worldwide. The insurance industry is already counting the costs. In 1997 alone it had to pay out US$4.5 billion to cover losses, and the total bill that the world's economies were forced to foot amounted to US$30 billion.

1998 was a year of extreme weather on a frightening scale. In January Canada experienced its worst ice storm in living memory. In February and March more than 1000 forest fires raged through Indonesia. Two months later 10,000 forest fires destroyed parts of Mexico, leaving at least 50 million people choking in smoke. In April the UK was affected by the heaviest rainfall on record but this pales in comparision to the massive flooding in Eastern Russia in June, which left 50,000 people homeless. July was declared the hottest month in world history. In August flooding in Seoul, Korea was the worst for almost 80 years. More than 200 people were killed and more than 80,000 made homeless. In China the Yangtze River reached its highest levels for 44 years and flooding affected 240 million people.

Since 1995 the world's governments have been meeting to monitor climate change and to agree a course of action to effect a global clamp-down on pollution. Few of the nations are prepared to make the severe cuts in fossil-fuel use that are necessary to halt climate change. That's why Friends of the Earth believes each and every one of us must do all we can to cut down on our polluting habits now to guarantee a future for our grandchildren. Because as well as causing climate change, pollution is also responsible for some pretty alarming alterations in the upper atmosphere around the ozone layer.

The ozone layer; what's eating it?

In chapter one you read all about ozone, a gas that is poisonous at ground level. High in the sky, some 25km above the ground, a fine layer of ozone surrounds the planet, protecting us from the sun's rays. This layer is crucial to life on earth. It soaks up almost all of the sun's damaging ultraviolet (UV) light, which causes skin cancers and eye diseases, and harms plants and animals. If the ozone layer were to disappear the sun's UV light would sterilise the surface of the planet, destroying everything except life forms in the deepest parts of the oceans.

In 1985 scientists found a hole in the ozone layer. This hole lies above Antarctica and is getting bigger all the time. Right now, it's reckoned to be as big as the US and as deep as Mount Everest is high. That's one hell of a hole! And it's not just the area above Antarctica that's affected. The ozone layer is thinning over parts of Britain and Europe, too. And what's eating it? Yep, you guessed it; human-made pollutants. So far, about 10 per cent of the earth's ozone shield has been destroyed.

Chloroflurocarbons (CFCs) are probably responsible for destroying much of the 'missing' ozone layer. These substances were invented, more or less by accident, in 1928 and were first used as the working fluid in fridges and later in air-conditioning units. They were then used to provide the spraying power in aerosols, used to puff up the foam for polystyrene cups and hamburger cartons and to clean computer circuitry. They drift upwards into the stratosphere, where they react with the sun's rays to literally eat away ozone. They remain (active and harmful) in the stratosphere for up to 111 years.

The production of new CFCs is banned in Britain, but they are still used by some international companies in other countries. There's also an illegal market in CFCs – so effective has their ban been! Smuggling CFCs into Miami is almost as big a business as drug smuggling. It's reckoned that some 20 million pounds of the chemicals appear to be smuggled into the US every year, partly because 100 million American air-conditioned cars have been built to use them!

Hydrochlorofluorocarbons (HCFCs) have been developed as a 'safer' alternative to CFCs and are replacing them for some uses. But HCFCs still destroy ozone slowly, so they are not a good alternative. Other chemicals that destroy ozone include:

- carbon tetrachloride, used in pesticides and dry-cleaning fluids – now banned in some parts of the world
- methyl chloroform, used in some aerosols, glues, dry-cleaning and industrial solvents. This chemical has been phased out for these uses
- methyl bromide. Another ozone-depleter, it isn't yet banned and is used as a pesticide on strawberry farms.

Developed countries around the world have made agreements to curb the use of ozone-destroying chemicals, which is why some of them are either banned or being phased out of use. However, the use of such pollutants in developing countries will be allowed until the year 2010; a worring thought when it's been estimated that up to 150,000 people will go blind each year for every 1 per cent decrease in ozone.

So there you have it. Pollution isn't just a dirty word; it's having a disastrous effect on our planet, big time. It's reckoned that millions of cases of skin cancer (not to mention eye problems) will occur as the ozone layer disappears and, if climate change continues unchecked, drought and famine will be a part of everyday life – for all of us, in all parts of the world.

Stopping the clock of doom

It's not too late to do something about it, though. The ozone layer will recover if we all use less ozone-destroying substances. However, if these were all banned tomorrow, it would be 40 years until the ozone layer healed. And every year that we continue to use ozone-destroying chemicals delays its recovery by nearly another four years. Industry must develop new, ozone-friendly chemicals to replace them as soon as possible.

On the climate-change front, the outlook is equally encouraging – as long as we change our ways! The IPCC have said global cuts in CO_2 emissions of around 60 per cent will be necessary by 2050 if climate change is to be kept at a level that the earth can cope with. That means that industrialised countries must cut their CO_2 emissions up to 90 per cent to average that target. Whether this is possible or not depends to some extent on you – yes, YOU! Because if we all commit to doing our bit, we will take the heat off the planet by using less energy – and wasting less energy too! There's not a moment to lose.

This is our only chance. If we all work together we can make the earth a cleaner place and secure a happy, healthier future for the world.

Pollution Busters!

What you can do personally

- find out if local factories are part of international firms. Then write and ask them whether they are continuing to use CFCs anywhere else in the world, even though these chemicals are now banned in the West
- write to your local MP and ask for her/his support in banning all CFCs and related greenhouse gases. Their use is now banned in aerosols but they're still used in fridges and air-conditioning systems. Industry must make safe alternatives to them – now!
- give aerosols the big E! Although they don't contain CFCs any more, they do contain other polluting chemicals and can't be recycled
- when your family needs a new fridge make sure you choose one that contains reduced levels of CFCs. And don't just dump your old fridge. If you can't sell it on, give it away to a charity. Or call your council and/or the fridge manufacturer and ask them to remove the old CFCs from it. These can (and should) be recycled!
- curb your car use. As you read in chapter two, cars are the single biggest source of excess carbon dioxide and produce other greenhouse gases, too. Car sharing the school run, for example, effectively cuts in half your share of the air pollution per journey and the cost of petrol – or better still, walk to school.

Conclusion

OK, so now you know the bad news: people all over the world are suffering from the effects of air pollution, contaminated land, polluted water and polluted food; toxic substances are being dumped in 'time-bomb' land-fill sites that threaten water supplies for hundreds or thousands of years; our seas are polluted; and now, to cap it all, the global environment we depend on is at risk from climate change and ozone depletion – and all because of pollution.

The good news is that there is a solution – and we all have a part to play in it. As we've seen, the car industry can make more fuel-efficient, less polluting cars, and we could all use our cars less in favour of more energy-efficient forms of transport, such as buses, bikes and trains. The chemical industry could introduce safer alternatives to replace the most dangerous persistent, gender bending chemicals, and we can use our consumer power to encourage them. Water companies could process sewage so that it is harmless and stop dumping sewage in the seas, and we could be more responsible about the waste products we flush down our sinks and toilets! We can buy organic food grown without the use of pesticides, growth promotors and antibiotics, and help reduce our impact on the planet in this way. Industry can generate energy less wastefully, and we can use that energy in our homes more efficiently.

Encouragingly, an international effort is already under way to clean up the planet. Since the 1992 Earth Summit the world's governments have begun meeting regularly (in New York and Japan in 1997) to discuss 'Agenda 21', an internationally agreed action plan for the future to tackle the threat of climate change and bring about sustainable development. Agenda 21 is about sustainability; reducing the amount of environmental damage we're doing to a level the planet can cope with (now and for ever!), so that our children and grandchildren can still enjoy life as we do. It also means sharing the earth's resources with people in poorer countries, to help improve their standard of living. Governments have also met each year since 1995 to discuss reductions in emissions of carbon dioxide, the main gas responsible for causing climate change.

Most countries are now in agreement that tighter anti-pollution restrictions are desperately necessary. It's just that few political leaders want to impose exactly what's necessary on their own countries for fear of losing their power. And governments often don't have (or choose not to have) much say over multinational companies that operate across the world. These companies are hugely powerful and sometimes exploit the differences between different countries' laws. Some locate their factories in the countries with lower environmental standards, where they can get away with producing filthy pollution and exploiting the local workers. For example, the oil companies that try so hard to appear clean and green in the UK have been responsible for serious pollution problems in other parts of the world. And as mentioned in chapter seven, they have put up serious opposition to adopting carbon-dioxide cuts and other pollution-reducing measures; in effect, putting profits before people and the planet.

In the last 100 years of life on earth we have done enormous damage to the planet but it is not irreversible. And in the last 10 we have gone further to slow down our polluting ways than ever before. The planet can heal itself, but we have to let that happen.

That's where you come in. Stay informed. When you are given the opportunity to vote, use it well. Find out which political party has the best environmental policy for the long-term good of the planet. Use your spending power carefully. Mega corporations will adopt cleaner, more ethical practices if they can be shown it will be profitable. And spread the word!

Appendix A
More Things You Can Do to Stop Pollution

OK, so you on your own may not be able to clean up the oceans or stop the destruction of the earth's ozone layer. As you've just read, even the most powerful nations in the world don't seem to be able to do that just yet (though they could try harder!). There are, however, many ways you can personally commit to making less impact on the planet. Here are a nifty 50 more pollution busters that you can do at home and at school, on your own and with your friends and family.

1. Turn off the TV and go and read a book instead! About two power stations are needed just to operate Britain's 38.3 million household TV sets for just one hour.
2. Stop wasting energy! Switch off your stereo, TV or video when they're not being used. In 1989 Friends of the Earth calculated that TVs on standby use more than £12 million of electricity a year; that's enough

to provide all the electric power to a town the size of Burnley or Basingstoke!

3. Replace the light-bulbs in your bedroom with compact fluorescent (energy-efficient) ones, instead. They produce the same light as ordinary bulbs but use up to 80 per cent less energy and last 8 times longer.

4. Invest in a set of rechargeable batteries for your personal stereo or CD player.

5. Better still, switch them to run on the mains whenever you can. Batteries are generally bad news because they take up to 50 times more energy to manufacture as they produce.

6. Whenever you have to make a short journey (under a mile) try to walk, cycle or bus it. Or go by skateboard or on rollerblades! Stay safe and get a friend to accompany you if you don't feel completely safe travelling on your own.

7. Be an environmentally friendly shopper. That means choosing products that have a less harmful impact on the environment (read chapter five again!).

8. Make-up and beauty products are often overpackaged to make them seem classier and more expensive. Before you treat yourself to some, think about how many layers of packaging there might be. How much is excess? Is it made of recycled materials? Can you recycle it, or parts of it, locally? If it doesn't have shades of green, then don't buy it.

9. Give aerosols the big E! Although they don't contain CFCs any more, they do contain other polluting chemicals and can't be recycled. Plump for refillable pump-action sprays or rolls-ons instead.

10. Invest in a big bright rucksack or holdall. It'll smarten you up and allow you to SNUB shop assistants and Say No to Unwanted Bags.
11. Only buy recycled paper products: note pads, jotters, printer paper, writing paper and envelopes, etc.
12. Ask your school to buy recycled stationery and other paper products.
13. Reuse your envelopes. You can buy sticky labels with cool designs from groups such as FOE, making reusing envelopes easy. Or make your own labels by simply sticking a piece of scrap paper over the address and stamp marks.
14. Make sure that whoever buys the loo roll in your home buys low-grade recycled paper. Rolls branded as recycled may be made from high-grade paper; loo roll is best made by recycling low-grade paper products instead, such as newspapers, which have few other uses once they're finished with.
15. When you, or someone else in your family, buys milk, make sure it's bought in glass bottles (which must be returned!) rather than plastic bottles and cartons. Milk bottles are refilled by the dairy. Refilling is better than recycling.
16. Sort out your wardrobe. Are any old clothes in there collecting dust? Then recycle them by taking them to a charity shop.
17. Remember the power of the pen. Write a letter to your local paper's letter page about a local pollution problem.
18. Write a letter to the prime minister asking for tougher laws to curb pollution and harsher penalties for polluters.

19. Set up a campaigning group at school to tackle pollution locally. Organise a school assembly on curbing car use to tell other pupils and teachers about how road traffic is polluting the planet.

20. Set up a paper-recycling scheme at school or college (and at work if you have a part-time job).

21. If you like gardening set up a 'green' garden at school or college. Plant native species of plants and trees in your garden and plant species that attract wildlife. Try growing organic fruit and vegetables that could be sold at school fetes to raise money.

22. Don't even think about buying peat for plant compost. In its natural surroundings peat acts like a sponge to soak up air pollution, so leave it where it is – it's nature's defence against global warming. Look out for peat-free compost.

23. Better still make your own compost by recycling kitchen waste and pet droppings. Follow Kruti's example in chapter five and invest in a wormery. You'll make rich compost for all your pot plants!

24. Turn down your central-heating thermostat – a 1°C reduction could lower your fuel bill by up to 10 per cent.

25. Make it your mission to turn your parents or flat-mates green (if they're not already).

26. Persuade them to fit your loft with at least 15cm of glass fibre or mineral wool and get them to lag all your hot-water tanks and pipes. This could save them up to £70 per year.

27. And while you're at it get them to draught-proof all doors and windows in your home and you'll be knocking up to £30 off their fuel bills.

28. Homeowners in the UK now have a choice of electricity suppliers. So ask your parents to choose a green electricity company, i.e. one that sells electricity from renewable sources. Friends of the Earth has a free *Guide to Buying Green Energy* to help them switch companies.

29. And if they're thinking of replacing their fridge, ask them to buy a new one with reduced CFCs. If they are getting rid of their old fridge, make sure the CFCs are safely removed from it. Your local council should be able to advise you on how this can be done.

30. If your parents are replacing any home appliances, ask them to choose energy-efficient models. Even if it costs a bit more now it will save money on your family's energy bills in the long run.

31. Don't boil enough water to make an army a cup of tea, just what you're going to use.

32. Use cooler washes and fuller loads in your washing machine.

33. Let that ironing pile up – yes, really! Set aside an evening each week to do it all in one go. A weekly ironing session uses up far less energy than lots of little ones. If you can coincide it with a *Friends* video sesh you'll be steaming!

34. Don't waste hot water; shower instead of taking baths. On average one bath uses up as much water as two and a half showers.

35. Don't waste cold water; or rather, any water at all. (If you've read chapter three you'll know that it makes sense to worry about water quantity as well as quality.) Put the plug in when you run water.

36. Mend any leaking taps around your home – now

there's a challenge! All you need is a monkey wrench and a bit of elbow grease.

37. If you're hoping for a major electrical appliance such as a stereo or TV for your birthday, make sure you choose the most energy-efficient model.

38. Never drop litter. Pocket it, or bag it, then bin it.

39. If you own a dog, don't walk it without a pooper scooper at hand. Whenever you scoop look around to see if there's any other dog's mess that you could clear up while you're at it. Think how much nicer our streets and parks would be if every dog owner was so thoughtful!

40. Better still, kick off a campaign for a dog-free zone in your local park. (In many parks dogs are given a free run. Dog-free zones, where they exist, are often too small for a lot of small children to play free from the risk of contracting toxocara poisoning.) Your local council may be very receptive to the idea, especially if it already has bylaws requiring dog owners to clean up after their pets.

41. Scan your local paper for notice of planning applications, especially developments that may pollute the local environment. If you spot a risky development write to the Head of Planning at your local council and ask her/him to object to the application.

42. If you're going out partying, organise a car (or cab) share to see you home safely.

43. Celebrate 5 November in a bonfire-free fashion. Throw an anti-fireworks party with lots of soup, popcorn and toffee apples, but with nothing burning! It's more pet friendly and you won't be a nuisance to neighbours.

44. Find out from the council where your nearest recycling facilities are...

45. ...and make use of them. But take note, making a special car journey to recycling points defeats the object of this exercise. So make sure you stop off at recycling points on other car journeys.

46. Keep an eye out for rubbish that has been dumped on the streets. Fly-tipping (as this is called) is unsightly, illegal and polluting. Report it to your council's Environmental Services or Cleansing Department and ask them to collect the festering rubbish pronto! Fly-tipping is unfair because it is the public who pays for the clean-up. If you catch a lorry, van or car tipping waste, take its registration number and report it to your council.

47. If you're an L-driver (or plan to become one soon), make sure you learn to drive with energy efficiency. And ask your parents to do so, too. Driving fast eats up lots of petrol, especially if you're revving really high in a low gear. On the other hand, driving slowly in a high gear uses lots of petrol as well – so don't drive over humps in third! You'll save money and petrol by avoiding driving fast and braking sharply, and switching the engine off whenever you pull up off the road – even if it's only for a minute or two.

48. Don't take driving lessons in an air-conditioned car. There's no safe alternative to the CFCs currently used for this purpose.

49. Think up some new ways you can help take the heat off the planet and...

50. Join Friends of the Earth. Ring 0582 485805 any time for more details.

Appendix B

35 Things the Government Should Do

1. Set tough standards on air pollution. (The UK government has set health standards for eight key air pollutants.)
2. Then see that they are kept to. This means enforcing all local councils and industry to meet these standards – heavily fining any that fail to do so! (The UK government has set targets to be reached by the year 2005 and has made local councils responsible for improving air quality to meet these targets. But they need to get tougher on councils who fail to do so.)
3. Stop all new road-building schemes. Improved road schemes only encourage more cars onto the road, so that even brand-new multi-lane bypasses and motorways quickly become traffic-jammed.
4. Make public transport more reliable, cheaper and comfortable so more people actually prefer to use it, rather than their cars.

5. Encourage rail use, particularly for long distance freight.
6. Reduce our need to travel so much.
7. That means banning the building of any more out-of-town shopping centres that can only be reached on wheels.
8. Encourage businesses and shops back into town and city centres!
9. Slap a tax on parking spaces at supermarkets. This would make stores keener to develop home-delivery services and also encourage people to walk or cycle to the shops.
10. Encourage people to drive less polluting cars by introducing a reduced road-tax rate for smaller, less powerful vehicles. Bigger, gas-guzzling cars should cost more to keep on the road to reflect the extra amount of pollution they pump out.
11. Encourage the oil industry to produce cleaner fuels. Recent legislation from Brussels has decreed that all fuel sold in Europe by the year 2005 must be much cleaner than it currently is. If governments put less tax on cleaner fuel now, so making it the cheapest fuel available, more people would buy it now, rather than in 2005, when they have to.
12. Introduce tougher laws preventing industry and farms from dumping dangerous toxins into the environment.
13. Protect our rivers, lakes and underground water from pollution by banning the most dangerous chemicals (especially gender benders, which threaten the future of humankind!) in areas where they might do damage.
14. Enforce industry to phase out the production of gender benders and other persistent chemicals.

15. Encourage organic farming. Stop subsidising farmers to use pesticides and other agrochemicals and put that money into sustainable farming systems instead. FOE also supports a tax on pesticides to reduce pesticide usage on farms.
16. Ban the can! Pass laws forcing drinks' manufacturers to sell their wares in refillable, returnable and recyclable glass bottles.
17. Encourage plastic and oil recycling.
18. Enforce all local authorities to recycle household waste. That means getting householders to separate their waste for collection. It also means the council must actually recycle the waste once collected.
19. Encourage manufacturers to stop over-packaging their products.
20. Insist that all schools and government organisations use recycled paper.
21. Stop councils incinerating rubbish, which releases polluting dioxins, heavy metals, dust, particles and acid gases into the air.
22. Insist that coal-fired power stations filter their fumes to remove most of the sulphur dioxide. This is a very effective way of reducing acid rain.
23. Invest in sustainable, renewable power sources (such as wind, water, wave and sun power) as alternatives to fossil fuels. They're cleaner, safer and, more importantly, won't run out!
24. Encourage owners to insulate their buildings properly, by offering them grants.
25. Introduce lower rates or property taxes on energy-efficient houses and so encourage more people to buy them.

26. Encourage electricity companies to get a percentage of their electricity every year from renewable sources.
27. Enforce local authorities to replace all the ordinary light-bulbs in local government premises with low-energy compact fluorescent lights.
28. Discourage shops from leaving their doors open all day. It wastes energy and creates pollution.
29. Encourage water companies to treat sewage effluent enough so that it's not harmful to swimmers and surfers.
30. Encourage industry to develop cleaner processes that use less resources and produce less pollution.
31. Make polluters pay! The cost of preventing or cleaning up pollution should be carried by those responsible for causing the pollution.
32. Make green cons illegal. This means prosecuting companies that deliberately try to mislead the public about their products' environmental performance.
33. Enforce companies to provide information on the full and lasting impact a product has on the environment.
34. Make sure that consumers get clear, accurate and full environmental information about all the products they buy. This will mean shoppers can make better-informed choices about the items they buy and so will boost their green power!
35. Enforce companies to provide detailed information about the polluting power of different makes of motor vehicles. Again this allows consumers to make an informed green choice when they buy their next car.

Appendix C
Spreading the Word and Using Your Voice

Although our own personal actions can make a difference in reducing global problems, you can boost your green power still more by shouting out about them for all the world to hear. Read on and you'll discover different ways in which you can use your voice – without raising it a single decibel!

Pen power

Writing a letter to people in power is the easiest way to make a protest and can be particularly effective in the war on pollution. Although many people often feel strongly about something, very few actually bother to write a letter about it. It's thought that each person who puts pen to paper represents at least 10 others who feel the same way. You may be able to convince decision makers of the need for change with just a few letters.

However, it's more likely that the authorities will only

act if they receive hundreds, or thousands, of letters from the public. You don't need to organise a letter-writing scheme on a huge scale. Thousands of signatures on a petition will show the powers that be how much backing your cause really has.

Ten top letter-writing tips

1. Explain clearly and briefly what you are concerned about.
2. Include some facts and brief background information, and then spell out exactly what you want the person to whom you are writing to do about it.
3. Be polite!
4. If you don't know the name of the person you're writing to, start off with 'Dear Madam/Sir' and sign it 'Yours faithfully'.
5. If you're writing to a large company you may not know who to address your letter to – so just write to 'The Manager' (of shops) or to 'The Director' (of industry). If determined, you can find out names of local managers and directors in the Chamber of Commerce Directory in your library.
6. Use your best handwriting. Better still, type your letter.
7. End with a specific request for further contact. In other words by making sure that your letter receives a reply.
8. If you can, fax your letter direct or, better still, use e-mail. People respond faster to e-mail and faxes than they do to snail mail.
9. If you don't get a reply within a week call to check whether they received your letter. Take notes of any phone calls you make. If you still don't get a reply,

write a reminder. Let them know that you're not going to go away!

10. Keep all your responses in the same file

What the papers say!

Writing to the letters page of your local paper is a great way to get your views heard. The letters page is one of the most widely read sections of any paper. A letter printed here can reach tens of thousands of people.

There's an art to getting in print, however. Basically it's best to keep your letter short and simple. Make one strong point, in less than 150 words or less; the most widely read letters are one sentence long! Get straight to the point. Include a few facts but don't pack in too many. Type your letter if possible and e-mail it if you can. And remember, if your letter isn't published straight away, write again – eventually one will be!

Strength in numbers!

Over the last 15 years action by green pressure-groups such as Friends of the Earth has brought about major changes in environmental policy. Thanks to their campaigning we've all become more aware of the environment and problems facing the planet. Frustrating as it may seem, the powers that be often only stop and take notice if they hear enough people saying the same thing. Or, to put it another way, when lots of people feel the same way they can influence decisions made by local and national government.

Join forces with school friends or other like-minded people in your area. Perhaps join a local Friends of the Earth group. It will be much easier to get things done if you get organised. The more help you have the easier your work should be and the more effective, too! The great thing about being in a group is that the work can be shared. Each member of your campaigning group will have a special role to play; ideally one that they are best suited to, such as organising people, fund-raising, looking after any money raised, organising stunts and dealing with the media. Even if you form a very small group, with just one or two friends, you should have more success working together than alone.

Ten tips for clever campaigning

1. Plan your campaign well. Before you start campaigning write down exactly what you hope to achieve and why. List the people or organisations whose ways you want to change. And make sure you get your facts right.

2. If your goal is a very big one, break it down into chunks that are easier to achieve. For example, rather than aiming to make your school pollution-free, go for a few modest pollution-reducing improvements, such as energy-saving measures and getting recycling bins set up around the place. That way you can celebrate sooner – before setting yourselves another goal!

3. Find out what other people think. Collect statements from people who agree with the aims of your campaign and then compile your results in a press release (see 'Using the media' below).

4. Don't underestimate your ability to achieve change. Obstacles will always be put in your way. If you can't get over the obstacle, go round it or under it. There's always a way of progressing your campaign or getting the information you need. If you need further encouragement, have another read of the case studies in this book. They're all real accounts from young women who've successfully taken personal action to stop pollution.

5. A quick call to your local paper or radio station can work wonders (see 'Using the media' below).

6. Create imaginative events – the media loves them! They don't have to involve lots of people. It's more important that they are eye–catching and the message is clear. Route walks, delivering documents, and even doing your own research can all be turned into good media events that will progress your campaign.

7. Always think ahead and plan what your next moves and options will be. Base these on facts; what you have found out from researching relevant documents (e.g. from the council). There is probably more useful information out there than you imagine. But always stick to the facts.

8. Get support by linking up with other groups. It's a matter of strength in numbers again!

9. Organise a public meeting to explain your concerns. Invite officials to answer their case to the public.

10. Stick at it. The campaign that wins is the campaign that believes it will win.

Seventeen-year-old Natalia Khazan has been an eco-activist in the Ukraine for five years. During that time

she's seen results but knows that real success only comes from 'real, hard and unrelenting work!'

'Our mission was to improve local air quality so we organised debates, public inquiries, street actions and fun festivals based around air pollution,' she explains. 'We met with the local authorities and representatives of central government, with academics and environmental officers, with eco-groups and activists.

'Because of its huge rocket plants Dnepropetrovsk was one of the USSR's "secret sites". It was really difficult to get any information about local pollution. Things have got a little easier since the Ukraine became a democracy, independent of the USSR, in 1991. We've learnt how to get a dialogue going with the powers that be and how to get the most from new democratic legislation. We produce two newsletters to help spread information and we've made TV and radio programmes about local pollution. Eventually one of the most popular local papers agreed to print regular info on air pollution affecting all areas of the town. The town's council has made air pollution top of its agenda. It's ordered researchers to determine the health and social consequences of air pollution in the town.

'We're targeting young people through festivals, concerts and kids' camps to continue our campaign. Right now I'm heading up a group devising a youth programme on a popular local TV channel, dedicated to environmental challenges of "the town and the world". It's got to appeal to both greenies and people that aren't environmentally aware at all; it's a challenge but we're ready for it.

'We don't believe that environmental problems are just technical ones. We really believe that we must change the consciousness of every person to avert an ecological crisis. It's more effective to campaign in a group because we have more time collectively than we ever could as individuals. Together we are very powerful!'

Using the media

Making the public aware of problems will spread your message and give more support to your campaign. And there's no better way of reaching people than through the media. A story in the papers, on the radio or better still on TV will be heard by thousands – and possibly even millions – of people.

The media can make a small story big news within hours. There's a canny knack of using the media to get results. Here are a few tips on getting good results:

1. Notify the media using a press release – preferably a single sheet of paper – to brief it about your story. Keep it short and snappy. Head it up with the words 'Press Release' and you'll make sure it lands on the right desk, rather than the bin! Make sure it tells them who, what, where, when and why in the first couple of attention-grabbing sentences. Include a quote that sums up your campaign message. This will save the media the trouble of interviewing you! And put a contact name and phone number on the bottom just in case it wants to follow the story up.

2. The media is always looking for an angle – that's media speak for the reason why a story is particularly interesting. Local papers will be keen to write about something that affects local people. National media might be interested if the story ties in with another issue that is currently hitting the headlines.

3. You'll have more success if you report good news, rather than bad. For example, stating that, 'A third of all locals would rather cycle or walk than go by car,' sounds more positive than saying, 'Most people are car potatoes.'

4. Phone and check whether your press release has been received. Ask whether the journalists are interested. This will give you a chance to fill in some of the information that there isn't room to put on an A4 sheet of paper.

5. Organise a stunt; anything that would make an interesting photo, video clip or radio story.

6. Involve a local VIP or celebrity. This will give the media a picture opportunity or sound bite that may mean the difference between getting coverage or not.

7. Try and organise your event before 11 o'clock in the morning and that way you might be lucky and make the lunchtime news!

The power of newspapers, radio and TV can help bring about changes in public opinion and government policy. The media can also be very useful in getting hold of information for you. Nurture your media contacts – don't pester them – and last but not least always remember that the media needs stories so you're not going to be wasting its time. And don't forget to keep copies of any press coverage your campaign receives; these will be your passport to a brilliant career!

Hot Contacts!

The following telephone numbers are public enquiry lines, open between 9 am and 5 pm, Monday to Friday.

The Prime Minister
10 Downing Street
London SW1A 2AA
Tel: 020 7930 4433

Department of Education and Employment
Sanctuary Buildings
20 Great Smith Street
London SW1P 3BT
Tel: 020 7925 5000
info@dfee.gov.uk
http://www.dfee.gov.uk

Department of the Environment, Transport and Regions
Floor 7/G10, Eland House
Bressenden Place
London SW1E 5DU
Tel: 020 7890 3150
http://www.detr.gov.uk

Department of Health
Richmond House

79 Whitehall
London SW1A 2NS
Tel: 020 7210 4850 (10 am to 12 noon and 2 pm to
5 pm, Monday to Friday)
http://www.doh.gov.uk

Ministry of Agriculture, Fisheries, and Food (MAFF)
Nobel House
17 Smith Square
London SW1P 3JR
Tel: 0645 335577 (helpline)
webmaster@int.maff.gov.uk
http://www.maf.gov.uk

Other useful addresses
The Advertising Standards Authority
2 Torrington Place
London WC1E 7HW
Tel: 020 7580 555
http://www.asa.org.uk

Alarm UK (Alliance Against Roadbuilding)
Southbank House
Black Prince Road
London SE1 7SJ
Tel: 020 7582 9279

British Wind Energy Association (BWEA)
26 Spring Street
London W2 1JA
Tel: 020 7402 7102
info@bwea.com
http://www.bwea.com

The Centre for Alternative Technology (CAT)
Llwyngwern Quarry
Machynlleth
Powys
Wales SY20 9AZ
Tel: 01654 702400
info@cat.org.uk
http://www.cat.org.uk

Community Recycling Network
Picton Street
Montpelier
Bristol B56 5QA
Tel: 0117 942 0142

Drinking Water Inspectorate
Ashdown House
123 Victoria Street
London SW1E 6DE
Tel: 020 7890 5956
dwi@dial.pipex.com
http://www.dwi.detr.gov.uk

The Energy Saving Trust
21 Dartmouth Street
London SW1H 9PB
Tel: 020 7222 0101
Efficient Energy Hotline: 0345 272200
http://www.est.org.uk

The Environment Agency
Rivers House
Waterside Drive

Aztec West
Almondsbury
Bristol BS14 4UD
Tel: 01454 624 400

Environmental Transport Association
Church Street
Weybridge
Surrey KT13 8RS
Tel: 01932 828 882
joining@eta.co.uk
http://www.eta.co.uk

Friends of the Earth
(England, Wales & Northern Ireland)
Underwood Street
London N1 7JQ
Tel: 020 7490 1555
info@foe.co.uk
http://www.foe.co.uk

Friends of the Earth Ireland
(Earthwatch)
20 Grove Road
Rathmines
DUBLIN 6
Tel: 00 35 1 497 3773/3744
foeeire@iol.ie

Friends of the Earth Scotland
Bonnington Mill
72 Newhaven Rd
Edinburgh EH6 5QG

Tel: 0131 554 9977
foescotland@gn.apc.org
http://www.foescotland.org

Friends of the Earth International
PO Box 19199
10006D, Amsterdam
The Netherlands
Tel: 00 31 20 622 1369
foeint@antenna.nl

Global Action Plan (GAP)
(Independent charity that offers practical step-by-step advice about what people can do to reduce their impact on the environment. Advice is geared towards the home, workplace and schools)
8 Fulwood Place
London WC1V 6HG
Tel: 020 7405 5633
all@gapuk.demon.co.uk
http://www.globalactionplan.org.uk

Greenpeace UK
Greenpeace House
Canonbury Villas
London N1 2PN
Tel: 020 7865 8100
editor@uk.greenpeace.org
http://www.greenpeace.org.uk

Independent Television Commission (ITC)
33 Foley Street
London W1P 7LB

Tel: 020 7255 3000
publicaffairs@itc.org.uk
http://www.itc.org.uk

London Campaign Network
228 Guildford Business Square
30 Great Guildford Street
London SE1 OHS
Tel: 020 7928 7220 (call between 2 pm and 5 pm,
Monday to Friday)

National Asthma Campaign
Providence House
Providence Place
Upper Street
Islington
London N1 0NT
Tel: 020 7226 2260
http://www.asthma.org.uk

New and Renewable Energy Enquiries Bureau
ETSU
Harwell
Didcot
Oxfordshire OX11 0RA
Tel: 01235 432 450/433 601
Fax: 01235 433066
nre-enquiries@aeat.co.uk
http://www.etsu.com/en_env

Oxfam
274 Banbury Road
Oxford OX2 7DZ

Tel: 01865 311 311
oxfam@oxfam.org.uk
http://www.oxfam.org.uk

Scottish Environment Protection Agency
Head Office
Erskine Court
The Castle Business Park
Stirling FK9 4TR
Tel: 01786 457 700

Soil Association
Bristol House
40–56 Victoria Street
Bristol BS1 6B4
Tel: 0117 929 0661
Fax: 0117 925 2504
info@soilassociation.org
http://www.soilassociation.org

Sustain: the alliance for better food and farming
94 White Lion Street
London N1 9PF
Tel: 020 7837 8980

Sustrans
(Engineering charity developing a national cycle network)
35 King Street
Bristol BS1 4DZ
Tel: 0117 926 8893
http://www.sustrans.org.uk

Tidy Britain Group
Head Office
The Pier
Wigan WN3 4EX
Tel: 01942 824 620

Transport 2000
Campaign for Sustainable Transport
Impact Center
12–18 Hoxton Street
London N1 6NG
Tel: 020 7613 0743
transport2000@transport2000.demon.co.uk

VIVA! (Vegetarians International Voice for Animals)
12 Queen Street
Brighton
East Sussex BN7 3FD
Tel : 01273 777 688
Fax: 01273 776 755
info@viva.org.uk
http://www.viva.org.uk

Waste Watch
Europa House
Ground Floor
13–17 Ironmonger Row
London EC1V 3OG
Tel: 020 7253 6266
Fax: 020 7253 6262
http://www.wastewatch.org.uk

Women's Environmental Network
87 Worship Street
London EC2A 2BE
Tel: 020 7247 3327
Fax: 020 7297 4740
wenuk@gn.apc.org
http://www.gn.apc.org

grab a livewire!

real life, real issues, real books, real bite

Rebellion, rows, love and sex . . . pushy boyfriends, fussy parents, infuriating brothers and pests of sisters . . . body image, trust, fear and hope . . . homelessness, bereavement, friends and foes . . . raves and parties, teachers and bullies . . . identity, culture clash, tension and fun . . . abuse, alcoholism, cults and survival . . . fat thighs, hairy legs, hassle and angst . . . music, black issues, media and politics . . . animal rights, environment, veggies and travel . . . taking risks, standing up, shouting loud and breaking out . . .

. . . grab a Livewire!

For a free copy of our latest catalogue,
send a stamped addressed envelope to:

The Sales Department
Livewire Books
The Women's Press Ltd
34 Great Sutton Street
London EC1V 0LQ
Tel: 020 7251 3007
Fax: 020 7608 1938

Livewire
from The Women's Press

Juliet Gellatley
The Livewire Guide to Going, Being and Staying Veggie!

Second edition, with revised and updated resources

So vegetarians are unhealthy? Worn out from spending all that time cooking complex dinners? Stupidly caring about animals while children suffer? RUBBISH!!!

Juliet Gellatley looks at how farm animals are kept – at live export, slaughter, fish farming, environmental destruction and diseases in meat.

But this superb, definitive book also shows how being veggie is more healthy and could feed the whole world. It gives tips for virgin veggies and suggests ways of dealing with hassle from parents, teachers, friends and enemies – with answers to the 40 most irritating questions you're bound to be asked!

Juliet Gellatley is the Director of Viva! – the dynamic vegetarian and vegan charity for adults and young people.

'Vegetarianism is now the way of the future . . . I chose Juliet [for the Linda McCartney Award for Animal Welfare] because she deserves more publicity for her work' Sir Paul McCartney

'Impassioned and comprehensive' *Books for Keeps*

'A useful and informative guide' *Good Housekeeping*

YOUNG ADULT NON-FICTION £4.99
ISBN 0 7043 4939 6

DATE DUE

0 5 SEP 2018			
			PRINTED IN U.S.A.